WILD AND WONDERFUL
FLEECE ANIMALS

Creative Publishing international

First published in the United States of America by
Creative Publishing international, Inc., a member of
Quayside Publishing Group
400 First Avenue North
Suite 300
Minneapolis, MN 55401
1-800-328-3895
www.creativepub.com

ISBN-13: 978-1-58923-578-6
ISBN-10: 1-58923-578-9

10 9 8 7 6 5 4 3 2 1

Library of Congress Cataloging-in-Publication Data

Carr, Linda, 1943-
 Wild & wonderful fleece animals : with full-size patterns for 20 cuddly critters / Linda Carr.
  p. cm.
 ISBN-13: 978-1-58923-384-3
 ISBN-10: 1-58923-384-0
 1. Soft toy making--Patterns. 2. Stuffed animals (Toys) 3. Fleece (Textile) 4. Animals in art. I. Title. II. Title: Wild and wonderful fleece animals.
 TT174.3.C385 2008
 745.592'4--dc22   2008000494

Technical Editor: Beth Baumgartel
Copy Editor: Karen Levy
Proofreader: Heather Dubnick
Book Design & Page Layout: Laura H. Couallier, Laura Herrmann Design
Cover Design: Howard Grossmann, 12e design
Illustrations: Linda Carr
Photographs: Jack Deutsch Photography

Printed in China

WILD AND WONDERFUL
FLEECE ANIMALS

with Full-Size Patterns for **20** Cuddly Critters

LINDA CARR

CD-ROM
INSIDE
FEATURES DIGITAL
PATTERNS (PDF)
FOR PRINTING

Creative Publishing
international

Contents

Making Fleece Animals

These soft and cuddly fleece animals are full of personality!

The magic is in the details—a well-placed stitch, a dab of color, a bit of extra stuffing, or a dot of powdered blush. Watch these animals come to life as you cut, stuff, and stitch. Colorful trims, pretty ribbons, sparkling eyes, and furry tails add the realistic finishing touches.

These wild and wonderful animals—from the jungle, the farm, the sea, and even your own backyard—are easy to sew. Fleece is an incredibly simple fabric to work with. The cut edges won't ravel, so you don't have to worry about frayed seams. Fleece can be fuzzy, nappy, or plush—but it's always soft and cuddly. It's available in a wide array of colors, weights, and textures, too, so you can have fun choosing your favorites.

These animals are perfect projects for first-time sewers, but all sewers will love how quickly and easily they go together. Even young children can make their own simple toys. Most of the animals are made with straight machine stitches and just a few hand stitches for the finishing touches. The instructions and illustrations (hand-drawn by the author) are easy to follow. On the CD-ROM that accompanies this book there are full-size patterns for all twenty animals.

Fabric and Supplies

To make the animals in this book, you'll need three basic supplies: fleece fabric, thread, and stuffing material. The color, pattern, and texture of the fabric give the animals their unique personalities. The stuffing creates volume and gives the animals shape and energy. There is a materials list for each project that includes any extras you need, such as yarns, eyes, or ribbons.

Fleece

Fleece is a fabulous fabric. It's inexpensive, easy to work with, and machine-washable. It's also great for the beginning sewer because it's very forgiving—the surface fibers hide sewing mistakes. Fleece is available in wonderful colors, patterns, and textures that are perfect for making wild and woolly animals of all sorts.

Fleece comes in a range of fibers, weights, and prices. Most fleece is made from 100% polyester, which is fine for these projects. Choose a fleece that doesn't stretch too much. To test the amount of stretch, hold the fabric between the finished edges (selvages) and gently stretch it. When you let go, the fabric should bounce back to its original shape. If it doesn't, or if it stretches completely out of shape, choose a different fleece.

Experiment with different weights, prints, and textures and see how the personalities of the animals change. Many fleeces are two-sided, which means they are fuzzy on both sides. Choose the side that you like best as the "right" side—the side that will show.

Try to find fleece that has a pill-resistant finish, so the fabric doesn't wear out quickly and your animal will live a long life! Check the end of the fabric bolt to find the fiber content and fabric finishes. To freshen up your fleece animal, just spot-clean it with warm, soapy water and a clean white rag. Dab fleece with clear tape to refresh the pile.

Thread and Yarn

To sew the pattern pieces together, you'll need cotton-wrapped polyester thread. If you can't find thread that is the exact color of your fabric, choose one that is the same hue or one shade lighter. Don't worry too much about thread color, however—the stitches tend to sink into the surface of the fabric and disappear.

To create eyes, noses, whiskers, and other facial features, you'll need embroidery floss. Be sure to keep a selection of colors handy. Yarn, in assorted colors, is great for tails and manes and other long and fuzzy embellishments.

Stuffing Materials

Polyester fiberfill is the best type of stuffing for most of the animals. It is inexpensive, doesn't clump or lump, and is nonallergenic. There are different grades and qualities of fiberfill, so work with the best quality you can find.

Some people like to stuff animals with dry rice. It's perfect for animals like Simon Snake on page 68 and Harriet Hedgehog on page 76. Animals stuffed with rice will be heavier—and a little more like their real-life counterparts. Rice is a good stuffing for reptiles, amphibians, and just about any other type of rugged animal. Only fill the animal about three-quarters full with rice to allow for movement and flexibility. Fiberfill is a better—and safer—choice when making an animal for a very young child.

Sewing and Embellishing Supplies

You don't need a lot of sewing supplies or tools to make these stuffed animals. A sewing machine that can sew straight and zigzag stitches does most of the work. You can even hand-stitch if you don't have a sewing machine. You probably already own most, if not all, of the other tools and supplies that you'll need to make every animal in this book.

SHARP SEWING SCISSORS: Choose a pair that fits comfortably in your hand. Don't work with paper scissors—they won't make a smooth cut.

EMBROIDERY SCISSORS OR THREAD SNIPS: Two sharp points make these small scissors perfect for trimming thread ends and seam allowances and for clipping corners and curves.

TAPE MEASURE OR RULER: You'll need at least one measuring tool to measure trims and seam allowances.

MACHINE NEEDLES: Start each project with a new needle. A universal needle, size 12/80 or 14/90, is a standard sewing machine needle that works well for most fabrics, including fleece.

HAND NEEDLES: You'll need a supply of all-purpose sharp needles and some long darning or embroidery needles to sew the stuffed animal closed and attach trims and eyes. Doll needles are extra long, between 3" (7.6 cm) and 4" (10.2 cm), and they're great for sewing eyes in place.

GLASS-HEAD PINS: Glass-head pins are easier to see and grasp than simple straight pins, which can get lost in the surface of the fleece. Standard pins are 1 1/16" (2.7 cm) long. Quilting pins are slightly longer, 1 1/4" (3.2 cm).

BLACK PERMANENT MARKER: Outline eyes and add decorative details with a permanent marker, such as a Sharpie marker. Keep both wide and fine points on hand.

DISAPPEARING INK FABRIC MARKING PEN OR A NUMBER 2 PENCIL: Transfer pattern markings onto the fleece before you start to sew with marks that have ink or lead that fades over time.

POWDERED BLUSH AND BLUSH BRUSH: Add shading and highlighting to an animal's face with powdered face blush and a brush (avoid cream blushes).

ACRYLIC PAINT AND A TOOTHPICK OR SMALL BRUSH: You can give embroidered eyes extra depth by dabbing them with a very small amount of paint.

Getting Started

Working with fleece is easy and practically goof-proof. There aren't any hard and fast rules about making these animals. As long as you enjoy the process, you're sure to love the results. There are only a few basic guidelines.

Working with the Patterns

The animal patterns are provided in individual PDFs on the CD-ROM that accompanies this book. To open the PDFs, you will need Acrobat Reader, a free program that can be downloaded at http://get.adobe.com/reader. The patterns are sized to be printed on 11" x 17" (279 x 432 mm/ANSI B) paper. The pieces for each project are clearly labeled and numbered for each animal. The ¼" (6 mm) seam allowances are included within the pattern, so cut each piece along the outside cutting line.

Make sure you check to see whether any of the pieces, such as inner ears, should be cut from contrast fabric. After you cut all the pieces for a specific animal, place them in a resealable plastic bag for safekeeping.

Laying Out the Pattern Pieces

The materials list tells you how much fabric you need. You'll probably have some fleece left over because fleece fabric is so wide. Save the leftover for another project.

Fleece has a right and a wrong side. It's usually easy to see the right side of a printed fleece fabric—the pattern is clearer on the right side and the colors are more vibrant. It's a little harder to determine the right side of solid-colored fleece. It doesn't really matter which side you choose as the "right" side for the outside of the animal's body, as long as you're consistent. Mark the wrong side of each cut piece with a strip of tape or pin so you don't get confused as you're working.

Fleece tends to stretch widthwise, or, in other words, from selvage to selvage. The selvage is the finished edge of the fabric. Keep that fact in mind when you lay out the pattern pieces. Position the larger pieces so they will stretch across the body of the animal (not along the length of the animal), as shown in the top drawing below. Smaller pattern pieces, such as the ears and tail, do not need to stretch, so they can be placed wherever they fit on the fabric. If the fleece has an obvious nap (fiber direction), lay out and cut all the pieces in the same direction. You can pin the pieces in place or draw around them with a black permanent marker, as shown in the bottom drawing.

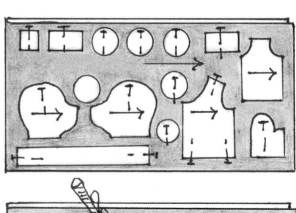

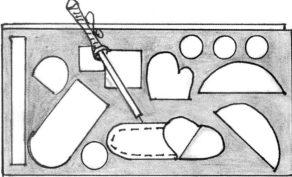

Marking

Working with a fabric-marking pen, pencil, or pins, copy the placement markings for eyes, ears, tails, darts, and other details from the pattern pieces to the wrong side of the fabric. To copy the placement points, which are small circles, insert a straight pin through the pattern marking. Open the fabric layers and mark the wrong side of both fabric layers at the spot where the pin goes through the fabric.

    Mark the dart-stitching lines the same way. Insert pins at the inside point and along the dart-stitching lines. Separate the fabric layers and mark where the pins go through the fabric. Remove the pattern piece and draw two lines to connect the markings so you have visible stitching lines.

Hand Sewing and Embroidery

You'll work with a sewing machine for almost everything. The only tasks that require hand sewing are sewing the animal closed and embroidering the eyes, nose, and mouth. Work with a simple slipstitch and regular sewing thread to sew the animals closed. Work with embroidery floss and the straight stitch or satin stitch to embroider the faces. Follow the pattern markings and how-to instructions to embroider the facial features.

SLIPSTITCH

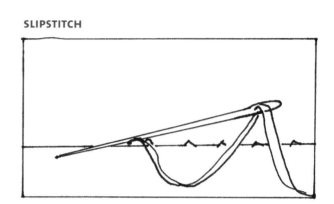

STRAIGHT STITCH

SATIN STITCH

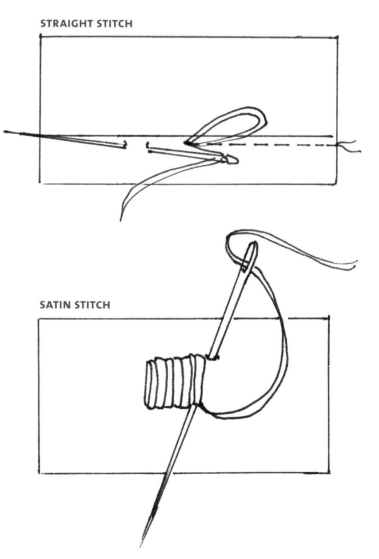

Machine Sewing

All of the projects are sewn with straight and/or zigzag stitches. Sew a row of practice stitches on a double layer of fleece so you can check the stitch length and tension. A standard stitch length of about six to eight stitches per inch (2.5 cm) is ideal for most seams. The thread should be smooth on both sides of the seam. If it isn't, check your owner's manual for instructions on how to adjust the thread tension.

All the seams, unless indicated otherwise, are 1/4" (6 mm) wide. Often, the edge of your presser foot makes a perfect stitching guide. Measure the distance from the needle to the edge of the foot to make sure. Sometimes you can adjust the position of the needle so that the presser foot edge is 1/4" (6 mm) away from the needle. Check your manual to learn how to adjust the needle position on your machine.

Many sewing machines have stitching guidelines in measured increments etched on the needle plate, so you can follow the 1/4" (6 mm) guideline as you sew. If your machine doesn't have guidelines, create your own stitching guideline by placing a piece of masking tape on the needle plate 1/4" (6 mm) from the needle. Once you have found or created your stitching guideline, align the edge of the fleece with it for perfectly straight seams and consistent seam allowances.

Fleece doesn't ravel, so you don't need any seam finishing. This fact alone makes fleece an easy and quick fabric to sew! Never press the seams with an iron, it could melt the fibers. Instead, finger-press the fabric to open the seams. You can also place a seam under a wooden block—or a heavy book, such as a dictionary—to smooth it and help it lie flat.

Stuffing Techniques

The stuffing techniques are slightly different for each of the fleece animals in this book, and each project includes its own specific instructions. Here are just a few helpful tips to keep in mind when working with polyester fiberfill.

Before you begin, separate the fiberfill, which comes in a large rectangular bundle, into handfuls for easier handling. Work with small amounts of stuffing to prevent lumpy surfaces. Often the head and legs are more firmly stuffed than the body so that the animal will be soft and floppy. Begin with the head, arms, legs (or tentacles!), and other appendages because you won't be able to reach them once you start stuffing the body.

As you work, from time to time, check the outside surface to make sure that it's smooth and that there aren't any lumps. Minimize creases and dimples by adding more stuffing and shaping the body with your hands. Don't overstuff—the stuffing will shift and settle into place.

When stuffing animal heads, hold the head in your hands. Add stuffing to make the shape symmetrical and round, like a baseball. Stuff the head so that it is firm, even if the animal's body is soft and floppy. After you have finished stuffing the head, add one or two small balls of stuffing to fill out the cheeks, nose, or other shaped parts of the face. You don't need to stuff the ears or tails.

If your animal has feet or paws, stuff those parts so that they are firmer than the body. One great way to make a realistic floppy foot or paw is to wrap drapery weights with fiberfill and insert one into each foot or paw. If you want to be able to position the animal so that it sits, don't add stuffing near the joints. Leave those areas empty so the limbs can bend easily.

All About Faces

The realistic expressions on the faces of these animals give them their personalities. Sometimes, creating a great facial expression is as simple as circling plastic eyes with a permanent marker or pulling your embroidery stitches a little tauter to shape a nose or snout. There are instructions for making the face of each animal in the book, but here are a few extra tips for making fabulous faces.

Eyes

You can make animal eyes with embroidery stitches, flat or ball buttons, or purchased plastic eyes. If you are sewing a gift for an infant, avoid buttons. Instead, substitute short, straight embroidery stitches or plastic eyes. Plastic eyes lock inside the head, so they are very safe.

BUTTON EYES

If you attach sew-through and ball buttons flat to the animal face, they will appear to pop slightly, as they do on Peter Panda on page 80 and Wally Walrus on page 102. The button eyes are backed with a fabric patch so they stand out. Simply sew them on top of the patch, through the head, the same way as you would sew a button onto clothing.

To sink button (or plastic) eyes slightly to create shape—as on Patrick Puppy on page 22, Rosie Rabbits on page 26, and Petunia Pig on page 52 —sew through the stuffed head between the eyes. Thread a long darning or doll needle and knot the thread end. Catch the inside of one button (or the fabric near the button) with two or three stitches and run the thread to the other eye. Pull the thread taut and repeat. Knot the thread. Add greater dimension by drawing around the eyes with a permanent marker.

PLASTIC EYES

Plastic eyes lock into place inside the head. Follow the instructions on the package. After the eyes are in place, with or without eyelids, and the head is stuffed, you'll want to sink the eyes slightly by sewing through the head—just as you would for button eyes. Outline the visible area around the plastic eye (the area not hidden by eyelids) with a black permanent marker.

EYELIDS

Eyelids are simply extra pattern pieces, hand-sewn to the face with very small straight stitches. The placement for the eyelids is marked on the pattern piece for each animal that has them. Follow the instructions for the project.

Noses and Mouths

The shape of the pattern pieces gives overall shape to the nose and mouth, but a few well-placed embroidery stitches will create even greater impact.

Pull the stitches taut, but not tight. In some cases, pulling the mouth stitches through the inside of the animal's head helps create a more pronounced snout, as for Catie Cat on page 18 and Hanna Horse on page 44. For satin-stitched noses, the number and consistency of the stitches create the round shape.

You can add freckles with a permanent marker. You'll find specific directions in the project instructions for each animal.

Backyard Animals

These familiar favorites, just like their real-life counterparts, are a lot of fun!

You can find ideas and inspiration for fleece animals right in your own backyard. Just watch your family's playful puppy run for a ball or your silly kitten bat at falling leaves. Track a fuzzy centipede on a lazy summer day. Keep a lookout for baby rabbits as they dart from shrub to shrub. You'll be surprised how many tiny, hopping frogs you can spy after a warm, spring shower!

It's easy to make a soft and cozy menagerie of everyday creatures. Just take out your sewing machine and get started. You can create realistic animals in solid or muted colors or sew fantasy animals in bright and cheery colors. These lovable critters are easy to sew and require only a small amount of fabric. You'll have as much fun making them as your child will have playing with them—indoors and out.

Catie Cat

This friendly, huggable kitty sits straight up. You can almost
hear her purring as she waits to jump into loving arms.

MATERIALS

eight pattern pieces

- ¹/₃ yd. (30.5 cm) fleece
- thread
- eyelash yarn
- scrap of white felt
- two animal eyes
- polyester fiberfill
- embroidery floss
- black marker
- ³/₄ yd. (68.5 cm) ribbon
- hand needle

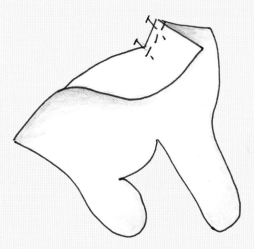

1 Pin and sew the body darts with right sides together.
Finger-press the darts open.

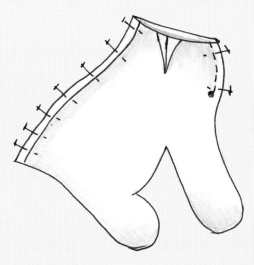

2 Pin and sew the body back and front seam to the marking
with right sides together.

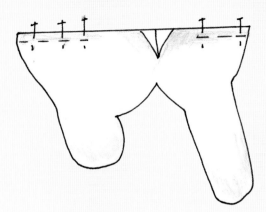

3 Pin and sew the underbody darts and finger-press open. Sew across the top from each end to the center markings with right sides together. Leave center open.

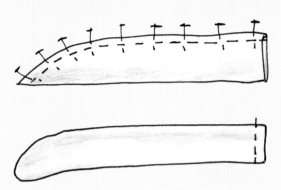

4 Pin and sew the tail with right sides together. Reverse and baste the end closed.

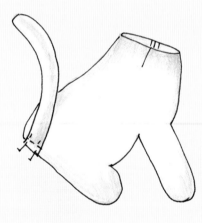

5 Pin and sew the tail to the center back of the body at the marking.

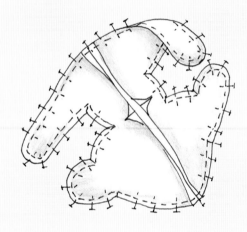

6 Pin and sew the entire underbody to the entire body with right sides together and tail tucked inside.

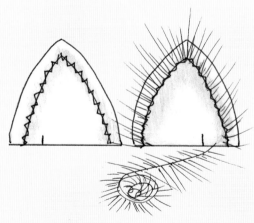

7 Zigzag-stitch the wrong side of the inner ear onto the right side of the outer ear. Hand-sew eyelash yarn over the stitches. Clip/slash each ear ⅛" (3 mm) at marking.

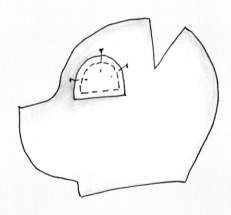

8 Sew eye patches over the eye-placement markings on the wrong side of each head side.

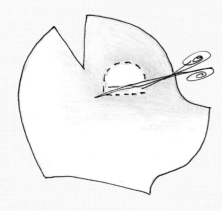

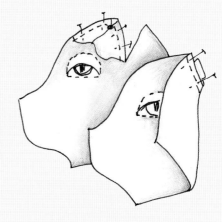

9 On the right side, slash above the bottom edge of the eye patch, just above the stitching. Push the lid up and insert a snap-in eye over the felt.

10 Pin the ears to the head sides with right sides together. Pivot ear at the slash. Pin and sew the head darts closed, catching the ears in the stitching.

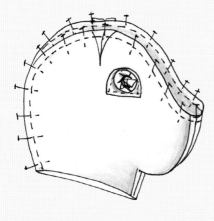

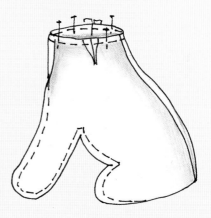

11 Pin and sew the center front chin seam with right sides together. Pin and sew the head center to the head sides with right sides together. Reverse.

12 Insert the head into the body with right sides together. Pin and sew the neck seam. Reverse. Stuff head firmly.

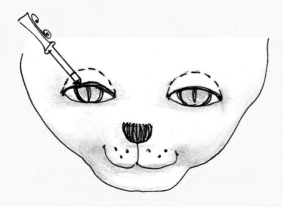

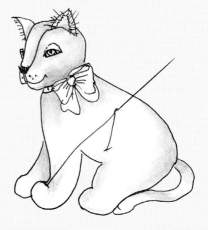

13 Sink the eyes by sewing through the head. Satin-stitch the nose and straight-stitch the mouth with embroidery floss following the markings. Outline the eyes and add freckles with black marker.

14 Stuff the body and hand-sew it closed. Fold up the bottom of the front paws and take two to three stitches to hold them in place to form joints. Tie a ribbon around the cat's neck.

Patrick Puppy

Ready, set, go! This loyal puppy looks ready for action. His softly stuffed body makes it easy for small hands to carry him everywhere.

MATERIALS

seven pattern pieces

- ¹/₂ yd. (45.5 cm) fleece
- thread
- two animal eyes
- polyester fiberfill
- embroidery floss
- scrap of pink felt for tongue
- black marker
- ³/₄ yd. (68.5 cm) ribbon
- hand needle

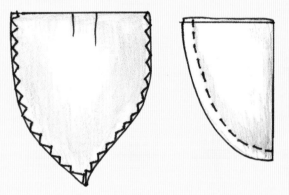

1 Zigzag-stitch the edges of the ears, except for the straight edges. Fold a tuck in the center and sew across the edge. Fold the tail in half with right sides together. Sew. Reverse the tail.

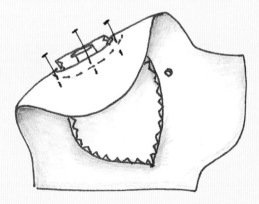

2 Insert one ear into each slashed opening on the head sides. Pin and sew.

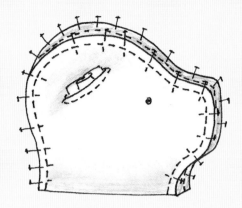

3 Pin and sew the center head to the head sides with right sides together. Clip the chin curve.

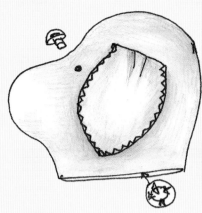

4 Insert purchased animal eyes at markings, following package instructions.

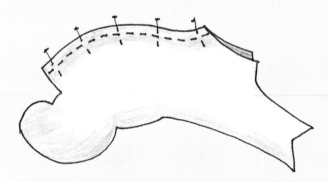

5 Pin and sew the upper body center back seam with right sides together.

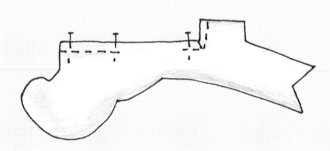

6 Pin and sew the underbody seam between markings with right sides together. Leave the center unstitched.

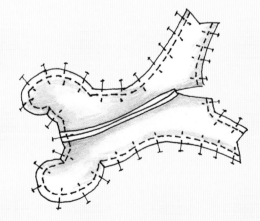

7 Pin the tail at the marking. Pin and sew the upper body to the underbody with right sides together, catching the tail in the seam. Leave the front edge of the front paws unstitched.

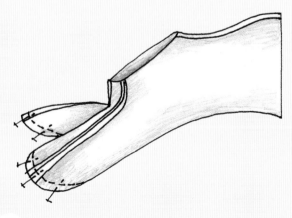

8 Fold the front paws so the seams are together. Pin and sew.

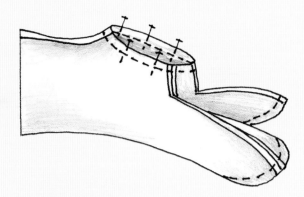

9 With right sides together, insert the head into the neck opening. Pin and sew. Reverse the puppy. Stuff the head and front paws firmly.

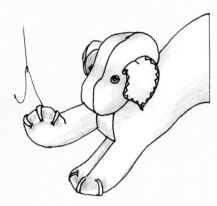

10 Take three straight stitches over the edge of the front paws with embroidery floss. Pull taut, but not tight, to shape.

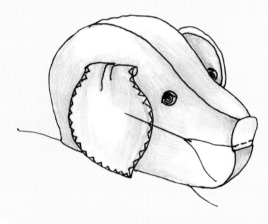

11 Hand-sew the upper edge of the tongue to the face at the marking. Fold the tongue over the stitches and tack in place on wrong side. Satin-stitch the nose at markings with floss.

12 Straight-stitch from the nose to the top of tongue and pull tight. Stitch from center to side mouth markings, stitching through the head. Take finishing stitches on each side and knot the ends.

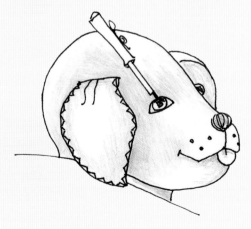

13 Darken and outline the eyes and dot in freckles with permanent marker.

14 Stuff the rest of the puppy and hand-stitch the opening closed. Tie a ribbon bow around the puppy's neck.

Rosie Rabbits

Soft and sweet, this rabbit family will be right at home on a bed or on
a rocking chair—or nestled in their own cozy blanket burrow!

MATERIALS

LARGE RABBIT OR SMALL RABBIT

- 2 yd. (2 m) of yarn for tail
- embroidery floss for nose and eyes
- polyester fiberfill
- powdered blush and brush
- black permanent marker
- hand needle

LARGE RABBIT

four pattern pieces

- 1/3 yd. (30.5 cm) fleece
- 8" x 12" (20.5 x 30.5 cm) fleece remnant
  for inner ear
- two 1/2" (1.5 cm) shank buttons for eyes
- 3/4 yd. (68.5 cm) ribbon
- 1" (2.5 cm) plaid ribbon flower (optional)

SMALL RABBIT

four pattern pieces

- 9" x 9" (23 x 23 cm) fleece remnant
  for body
- 3" x 4" (7.5 x 10 cm) fleece remnant
  for inner ear
- white paint
- 3/4 yd. (68.5 cm) ribbon
- 1/2" (1.5 cm)-wide pink ribbon flower

LARGE RABBIT

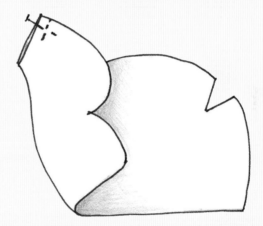

1 Fold the head darts closed with right sides together.
Stitch 5/8" (1.5 cm) at the top of the dart. Leave the rest
of the dart open.

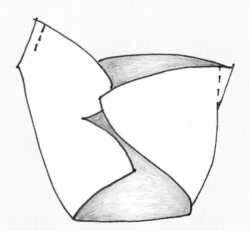

2 Sew the back darts and finger-press open.

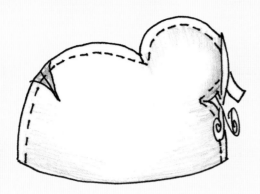

3 With right sides together, pin and sew the body at the upper edge. Trim the seam around the head. Clip the curve.

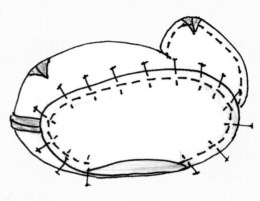

4 Pin and sew the rabbit bottom to the body, with right sides together. Leave a 3" (7.5 cm) opening for stuffing.

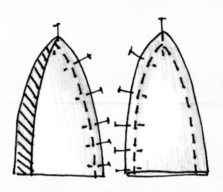

5 Pin and sew the outer ear to the inner ear with right sides together (the outer ear is larger than the inner ear). Reverse the ear.

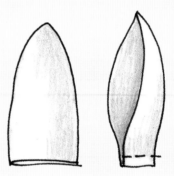

6 Fold the ears in half so the contrast fabric is inside the ear. Stitch across bottom edge.

7 Insert the ears into the dart openings. Hand- or machine-sew the darts closed. Reverse the rabbit. Stuff the head firmly.

8 Satin-stitch the nose with floss. Stitch back and forth through the head three or four times, at marked locations, to attach and sink the eyes.

9   To make the tail, wrap the yarn around your hand or a piece of cardboard several times.

10   Slip the yarn loops off and tie the centers with yarn. Cut the loops and shake to fluff. Trim yarn to form a round tail.

11   Add a small ball of stuffing to fill out the rabbit's cheeks. Stuff the body. Slipstitch the bottom closed. Hand-sew the tail at the marking. Tie embroidery floss around the neck to shape.

12   Outline the eyes with marker. Apply powdered blush to inner ears and cheeks. Tie ribbon around the rabbit's neck. Add flower, if desired.

SMALL RABBIT

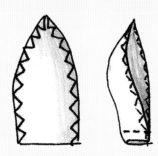

1   Follow steps 1, 3, and 4 for Large Rabbit. Pin wrong side of inner ears to right side of outer ears. Zigzag-stitch the perimeter. Follow steps 6 and 7 for Large Rabbit.

2   Stuff the head firmly. Satin-stitch the eyes and nose. Apply a dot of marker and white paint to the center of the embroidered eyes. Follow steps 9, 10, and 11 for Large Rabbit. Tie ribbon around neck.

Cindy Centipede

Every arthropod lover deserves a soft and colorful, crawly centipede. You can make this little creature from leftover fleece scraps of many colors.

MATERIALS

four pattern pieces

- five different colors of fleece remnants
- sewing thread
- 3" (7.5 cm)-diameter Styrofoam ball
- 3 yd. (3 m) cording
- fabric glue
- upholstery or buttonhole-twist heavy thread
- thirty to thirty-five pony beads
- 1 yd. (91.5 cm) ⅝" (1.5 cm)-wide decorative ribbon
- two pipe cleaners
- pencil
- one small and two large pom-poms
- two ball buttons for eyes
- embroidery floss
- powdered blush and brush
- hand needle

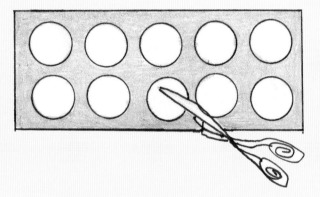

1 Plan the color pattern you like. Trace and cut forty-two body circles from different colors of fleece.

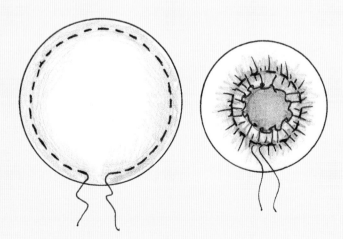

2 Run a gathering stitch around the perimeter of the head. Place the ball in the center and pull stitches to cover the ball. Secure with two or three stitches.

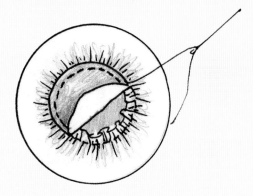

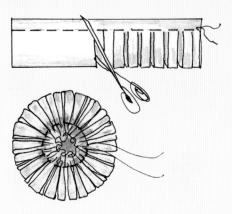

3 Hand-stitch the head back over the gathered edge.

4 Fold the first round "collar" in half with wrong sides together. Baste the edges together ¼" (6 mm) from the top. Cut slashes from fold to stitching ¼" (6 mm) apart. Pull the gathering to form a circle.

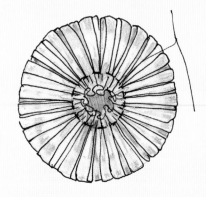

5 Repeat step 4 with the second collar. Hand-stitch the collars to the back of the head.

6 Cut ten 8" (20.5 cm) pieces of cord. Tie a knot in the center of each piece and knot the ends.

7 Apply a dab of fabric glue at each knot. Trim the ends.

8 With a long, doubled piece of heavy thread and hand needle, secure the thread at the center of the collar. Run the thread through the knot of one leg, the center of one circle, and one bead.

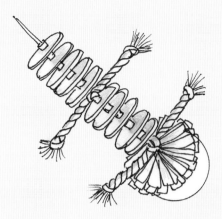

9 Continue stringing one circle and then one bead so there are five circles. Then run thread through the knot of the next leg. Repeat until you've threaded all circles and legs.

10 Tie a ribbon bow at the neck and the back end.

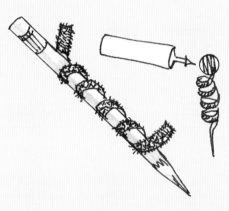

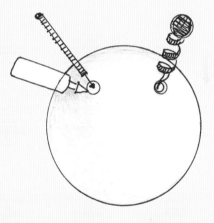

11 Cut pipe cleaner into 3" (7.5 cm) pieces and wrap both pieces around the pencil. Remove the pencil. Glue the large pom-pom to one end of each pipe cleaner.

12 Poke holes at the antennae markings through the fabric and into the Styrofoam. Fill the holes with glue and insert pipe cleaners.

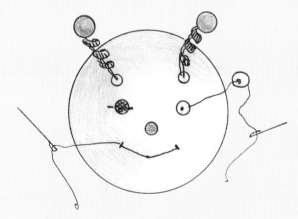

13 Stitch the button eyes at the markings. Glue on the small pom-pom nose and straight-stitch the mouth with floss following the pattern markings.

14 Apply blush to the centipede's cheeks.

Freddie Frog

Perfect at pocket size, this wide-eyed frog looks ready to hop from the swamp into your heart—or least into the little hands of a happy frog finder!

MATERIALS LIST

five pattern pieces

- ⅛ yd. (11.5 cm) fleece
- 4" x 6" (10 x 15 cm) contrast fleece
- two ⅝" (1.5 cm)-diameter snap-in eyes
- sixteen ¼" (6 mm) pom-poms
- polyester fiberfill
- embroidery floss
- glue

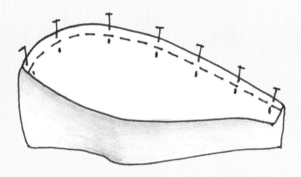

1 Pin and sew the head side to the upper body with right sides together.

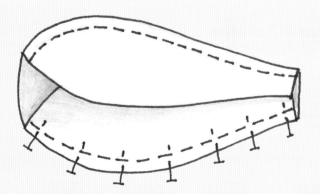

2 Pin and sew the remaining head side to the upper body with right sides together.

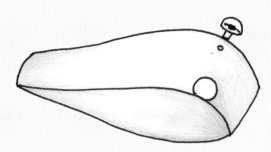

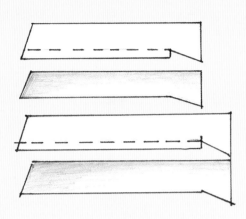

3 Cut two small holes with scissors in the upper body at pattern markings. Insert the eyes in holes and clamp them in place (refer to package instructions).

4 Pin and sew all four legs with right sides together, ending the stitching at the notch. Reverse and do not stuff.

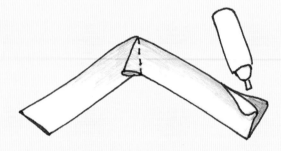

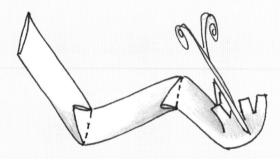

5 Glue unstitched hands together. Fold and stitch the darts at the leg markings.

6 After the glue is dry, cut three slashes along the hand markings.

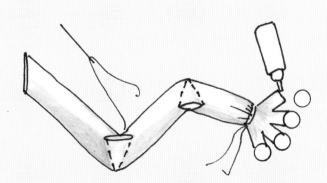

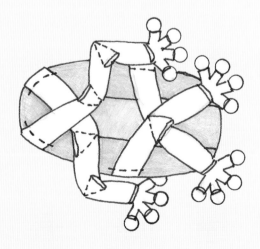

7 Wrap and knot the thread around the legs near the hands and pull tight. Finger-press the darts open and hand-stitch in place. Glue the pom-poms on top of each finger.

8 Pin and stitch the legs to the wrong side of the body at pattern markings.

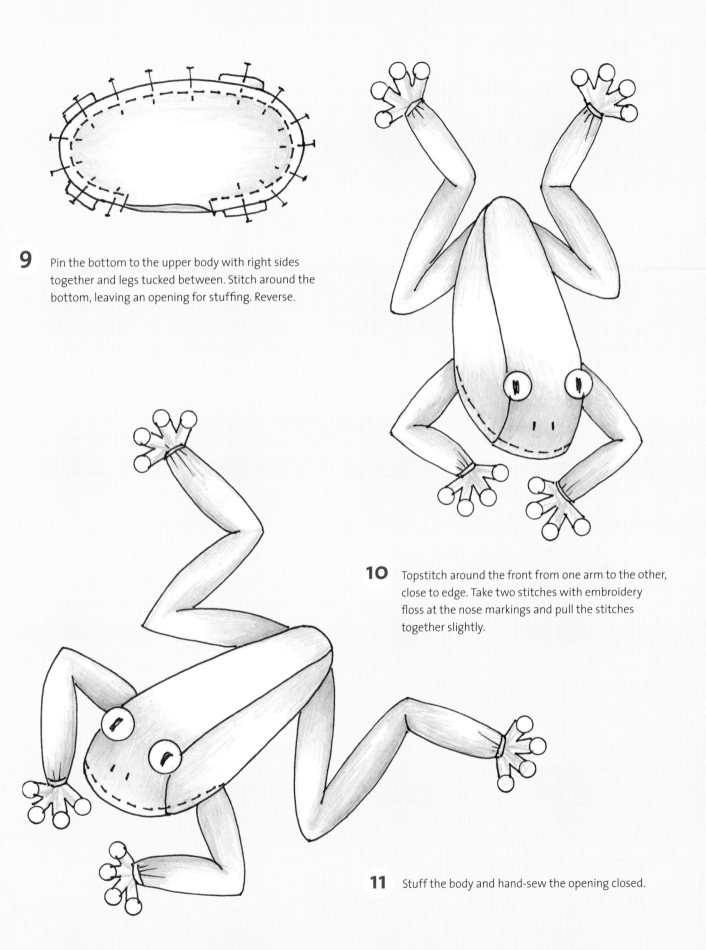

9 Pin the bottom to the upper body with right sides together and legs tucked between. Stitch around the bottom, leaving an opening for stuffing. Reverse.

10 Topstitch around the front from one arm to the other, close to edge. Take two stitches with embroidery floss at the nose markings and pull the stitches together slightly.

11 Stuff the body and hand-sew the opening closed.

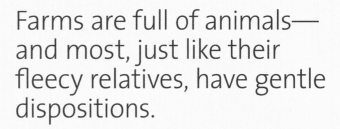

Farm Animals

Farms are full of animals— and most, just like their fleecy relatives, have gentle dispositions.

But you don't need to build a barn or pitch hay to have your own farmyard friends. Imagine a pink pig that's squeaky clean, a curly-haired lamb that will always follow you home, and a colorful spider that isn't the least bit alarming. You can make each—or all—of these endearing creatures and a duck and a horse, too.

These lovable animals love to play together, or you can give them each a wide, open space of their own on a bed, in a crib, or on a bookshelf or nightstand. They love attention and are designed for safe play for even the youngest farm-hands! To add an extra-special touch, make a saddle for your pony or add a purchased flower for your piglet. You'll find the instructions on pages 107 and 109.

Delilah Duck

One little, two little, three little quackers, or as many as you'd like
in as many colors as suit your décor. This darling duck is simple
to make—just an hour from start to finish.

MATERIALS

four pattern pieces

- ¼ yd. (23 cm) fleece
- fleece remnant for beak
- yarn
- thread
- polyester fiberfill
- two small pony beads
- hand needle

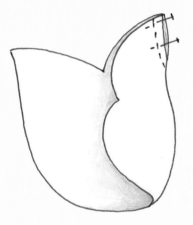

1 Pin and sew the top head darts with right sides together.

2 Tack several uneven pieces of yarn at the top of each dart.

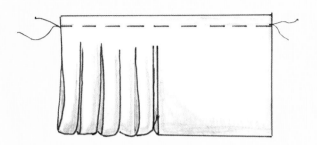

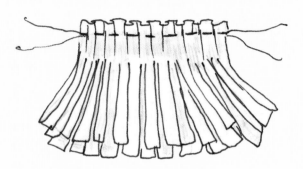

3 Fold the wings with wrong sides together. Baste across the tops. Slash from the fold up to the stitching every ¼" (6 mm).

4 Pull the basting stitch to gather the wings to fit inside the slashed body opening.

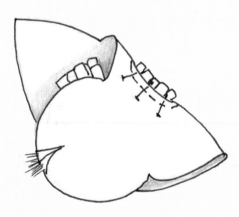

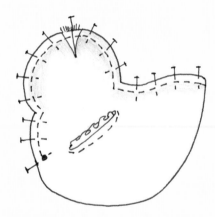

5 Insert the gathered edge of the wings into the openings and pin. Sew the openings closed, catching the wings in the seam.

6 Pin and sew the top seam from marking to tail end with right sides together.

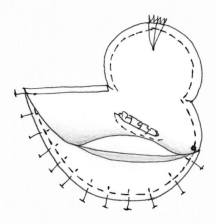

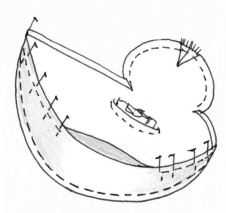

7 Pin and sew one side of the under body to one side of the body with right sides together.

8 Pin and sew the other side of the under body to the other side of the body with right sides together. Leave an opening. Reverse the duck.

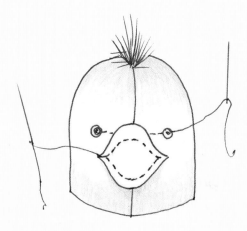

9 Stuff the head firmly. Sew beads at the eye markings, pulling the stitches through the head to sink the eyes slightly. Hand-sew the beak in place as shown.

10 Stuff the body. Hand-sew the opening closed. Tie thread around the neck to shape and knot the ends. Tack down the beak corners.

Hanna Horse

Horse lovers will adore this lifelike equine creature, who is quite at home in the family room, in the nursery, or alongside fleecy friends.

MATERIALS

six pattern pieces

- ½ yd. (46 cm) fleece
- 4" x 10" (10 x 25.5 cm) contrast piece of fleece for feet
- thread
- yarn
- two plastic eyes
- polyester fiberfill
- 1¼ yd. (114.5 cm) ⅛" (3 mm)-wide trim
- four ⅛" (3 mm) gold beads
- black permanent marker
- hand needle

For saddle and blanket materials and instructions, see page 107.

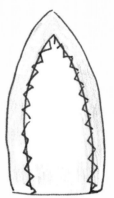

1   Zigzag-stitch the wrong side of the inner ear onto the right side of outer ear. Fold in half and stitch across the bottom.

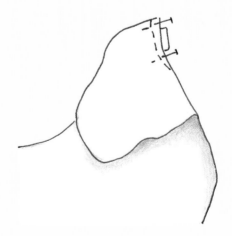

2   Pin the ears to the head with right sides together and ears pointing toward body. Stitch the head darts, enclosing the ears in the stitching.

3 Pin and stitch the back darts.

4 Cut the yarn into 5" to 6" (12.5 to 15 cm) lengths. Stitch the yarn along the top of the head, neck, and tail.

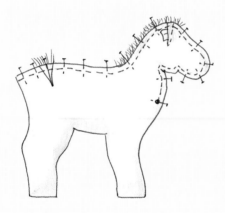

5 Pin and stitch the head and upper body with right sides together.

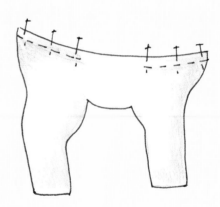

6 Pin and sew from front and back ends of the underbody up to the center markings with right sides together. Leave the center open.

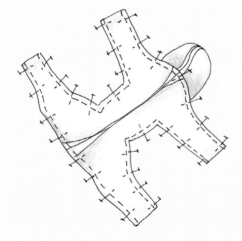

7 Pin and stitch the underbody to the body with right sides together. Leave the center unstitched.

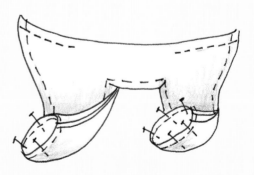

8 Pin and sew a foot bottom to each leg, easing the stitching to fit. Clip the curves.

9 Clip tiny holes at the eye markings. Insert the eyes through the body and snap tightly into place. Stuff the head firmly.

10 Hand-sew the eyelids over the eyes. Make straight stitches at the nose markings, pulling the thread through the head to shape. Knot the thread.

11 Make a stitch at one mouth marking and wrap the thread around the mouth to other side. Insert the needle through the head and come out at the original stitch. Knot the thread.

12 Wrap a 5" (12.5 cm)-long piece of trim around the nose and stitch the ends under the head. Wrap an 11" (28 cm) length of trim around the neck, in front and behind the ears as shown. Stitch the ends.

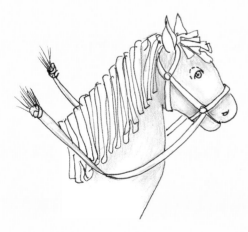

13 Stitch a 10" (25.5 cm) length of trim near the ears to make reins. Wrap opposite ends under the trim near the mouth. Sew gold beads to secure the trim at the crossings. Knot the rein ends.

14 Stuff the horse and hand-sew the opening. Outline the eyes at the lid edges with permanent marker.

Lulu Lamb

Textured or curly fleece is the perfect fabric for the top of this lovable lamb.
Make a whole family and let them graze in a special spot.

MATERIALS

five pattern pieces

- ½ yd. (45.5 cm) fleece
- ¼ yd. (23 cm) textured fleece
- small remnant of white felt
- thread
- two ½" (1.5 cm) ball buttons
- polyester fiberfill
- embroidery floss
- black permanent marker
- powdered blush and brush
- hand needle

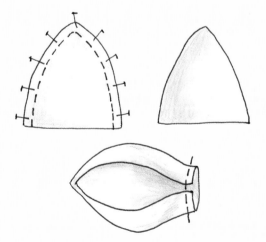

1   Zigzag-stitch the wrong side of the overbody pieces onto the right side of the lamb bodies.

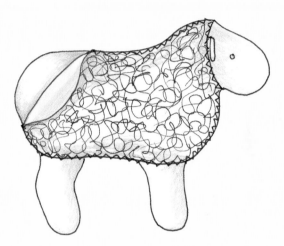

2   Pin and stitch the ears with right sides together. Reverse and stitch across the bottom. Fold the bottom edges to meet in the center. Stitch.

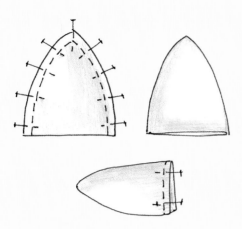

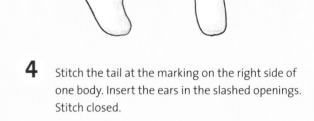

3 With right sides together, pin and stitch the tail. Reverse and stitch across the bottom. Fold the tail in half and stitch across the bottom.

4 Stitch the tail at the marking on the right side of one body. Insert the ears in the slashed openings. Stitch closed.

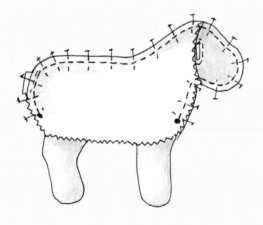

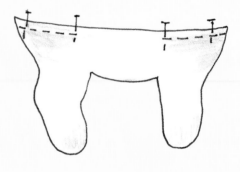

5 With right sides together, pin and sew the upper edge of the lamb between markings.

6 With right sides together, pin and sew the upper edge of the underbody pieces together between the markings on each end, leaving the center open.

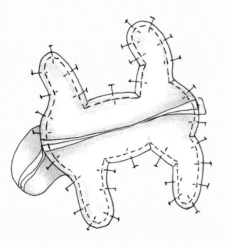

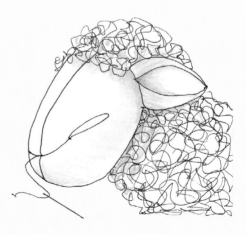

7 Pin and sew the underbody to the upper body with right sides together. Pivot at the corners and ease around curves. Clip the corners. Reverse and stuff the head firmly.

8 To shape the nose, stitch from each side dot to the center dot with floss and pull taut. Secure the stitches with two or three small stitches in the center—don't cut the thread.

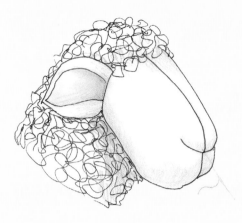

9 Working with the same floss, stitch from the center of the nose down ¾" (2 cm) and pull the stitch taut.

10 Stitch from the center to the side markings through the head to create the mouth. Pull taut. Secure the stitches with one small stitch at center front.

11 Stitch a button at each eye marking, pulling the thread through the head to sink the eyes. Secure the eyes with small stitches or knots. Add a small ball of stuffing to each check.

12 Stuff the legs firmly. Stuff the body lightly.

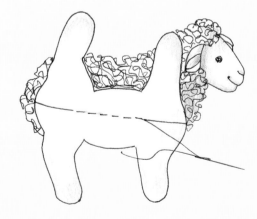

13 Hand-sew the bottom closed.

14 Outline the button eyes with black permanent marker. Dust blush on the cheeks and inside the ears.

Petunia Pig

She's so pretty in pink! It's hard to imagine this sweet piglet
ever wallowing in mud when she can lounge in luxury in
the comfort of a certain little someone's room.

MATERIALS

six pattern pieces

- ¹/₃ yd. (30.5 cm) fleece
- pale pink fleece remnant for nose
- thread
- one pipe cleaner
- polyester fiberfill
- two ball buttons
- faux flower
- hand needle
- pencil
- black permanent marker

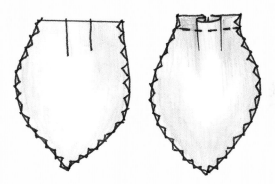

1 Zigzag-stitch around the outside edge of the ears. Fold the
tucks and baste across the top.

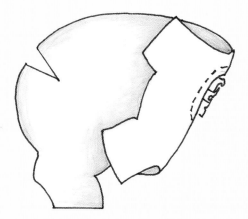

2 Insert the ears into the slashed openings. Pin and stitch,
catching the ends of the ears in the seam.

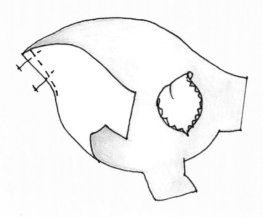

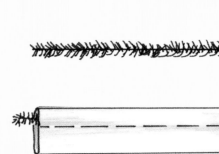

3 Pin and sew the back darts with right sides together.

4 Fold the pipe cleaner in half, leaving a loop and wrapping the ends together. Cover with fleece, wrong sides together. Stitch close to the pipe cleaner.

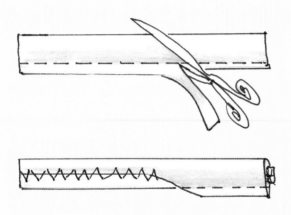

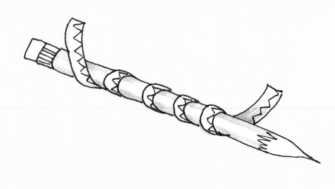

5 Trim close to the stitching. Fold the cut ends up and over the pipe cleaner. Zigzag-stitch by hand or machine through all layers.

6 Wrap the tail around the pencil, then slide the pencil out.

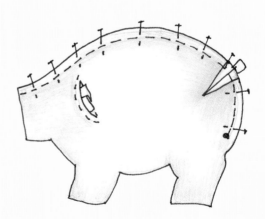

7 Baste the tail to the right side of one body back at the dart marking.

8 Sew the bodies together along the center back seam with right sides together. Catch the tail in the seam.

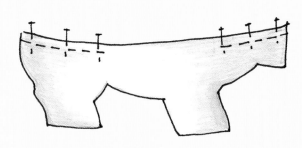

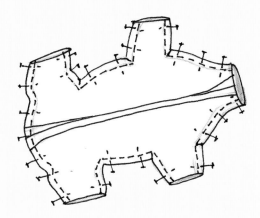

9 Pin and sew the underbody seam between the markings with right sides together. Leave the center unstitched.

10 Pin and sew the body to the underbody with right sides together. Leave the feet and nose unstitched. Clip the corners.

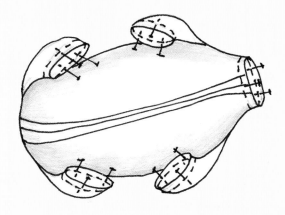

11 Sew the tucks in the nose with right sides together. Pin the nose and feet into body openings with right sides together. Stitch, easing to fit.

12 Stuff the head firmly. Sew the buttons at the eye markings, pulling the thread through the head to sink the eyes slightly. Finish stuffing and hand-sew the opening closed.

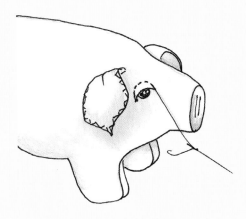

13 Hand-stitch the eyelids over the eyes.

14 Darken the lower rim of the eyes and the lower edge of the eyelids with permanent marker. Sew on the faux flower.

Sammy Spider

Here's the best way to invite a spider into your home. Custom-make one that has all of the wonder of a real spider but no messy web!

MATERIALS

five pattern pieces

- ¼ yd. (23 cm) fleece for the body
- two 5" x 7" (12.5 x 18 cm) fleece remnants in different colors for bottom
- ⅛ yd. (11.5 cm) striped fleece for legs
- scrap of white fleece for eyes
- thread
- ten pipe cleaners
- polyester fiberfill
- embroidery floss
- two black ball buttons or beads
- hand needle

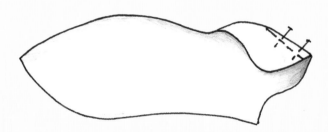

1   Pin and sew the mouth dart with right sides together.

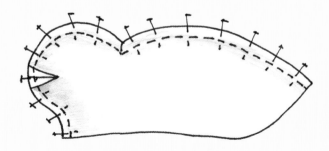

2   Pin and sew the front and top of the body with right sides together.

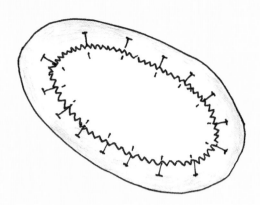

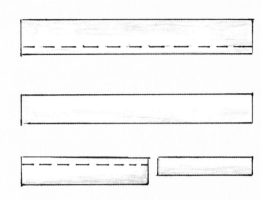

3 Center and zigzag-topstitch the wrong side of the underbody belly on the right side of the underbody.

4 Sew the long side of eight long and two short legs with right sides together. Reverse.

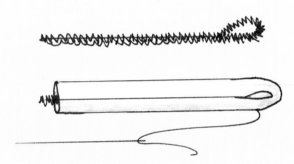

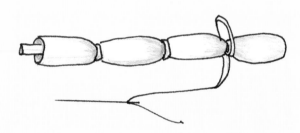

5 Loop and twist one end of each pipe cleaner. Insert one in each leg. Turn the fabric edges to the wrong side near the loops. Hand-sew the legs closed.

6 Trim the excess pipe cleaner. Wrap the thread tightly around the long legs at the markings to create joints. Knot the thread securely.

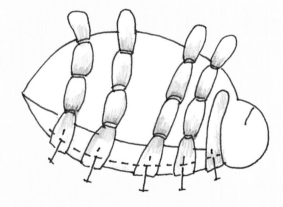

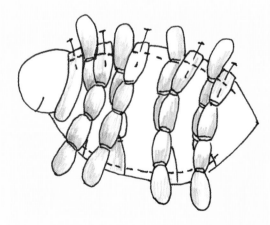

7 Pin and sew the unstitched end of the legs to the right side of body. Position one shorter leg near the head.

8 Repeat step 7 with the remaining legs on the opposite side of the body.

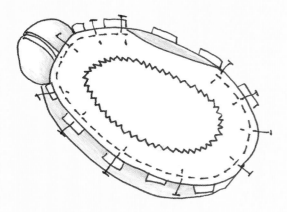

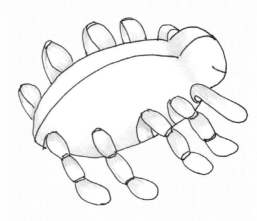

9 Turn the body right side up and tuck the legs inside. Pin and sew the right side of the underbody to the body, leaving an opening.

10 Reverse the spider and extend the legs. Stuff until moderately firm. Hand-stitch the opening closed.

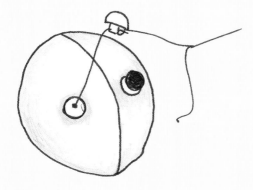

11 Cut two small white felt circles for eyes. Sew buttons through the felt circles onto the head at the markings.

12 Satin-stitch the nose. Straight-stitch the mouth over the dart stitching, anchoring stitches on each side and pulling tight to form a smile.

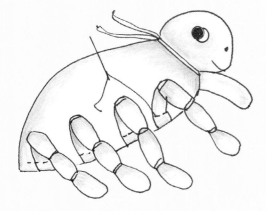

13 Wrap thread around the spider's neck and pull tight to shape the head. Knot securely. Hand-tack the legs close to the body so they extend up and outward.

14 Hand-sew the front legs to the bottom of the head, as in step 13.

Wild Animals

There's nothing to be afraid of! These animals may be wild, but they're sweet as can be.

From the super-simple snake to the slightly more challenging gorilla, there's something wild here for everyone. No matter what their natural temperaments might be, with a little affection they're easy to tame.

Notice how each set of eyes is different, giving each animal its own personality. The snake and hedgehog have small beads for eyes. The gorilla and tiger get their wild look from snap-in eyes that have a lifelike glow. The panda's eyes are simple buttons, but one hole is sewn with white thread to give them a twinkle.

One of the pleasures of sewing with fleece is that it doesn't ravel, so you can just cut strips to make furry arms or hedgehog spikes. All you have to do is sew and snip! Adjust the amount of stuffing, depending on whether you want a soft, bendable, drapable animal or one that stands alert and attentive, ready to explore the great outdoors.

Grover Gorilla

There's sure to be monkey business whenever this guy is around. Watch him swing from room to room and right into action as king of all fleece things.

MATERIALS

twelve pattern pieces

- ¼ yd. (23 cm) fleece
- 8" x 14" (20.5 x 35.5 cm) contrast fleece remnant
- thread
- polyester fiberfill
- two large animal eyes
- 1 yd. (91.5 cm) cording
- embroidery floss
- hand needle
- permanent marker

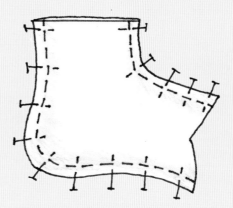

1 Pin and sew the top and bottom of two feet (but not the toes) with right sides together. Repeat for remaining feet.

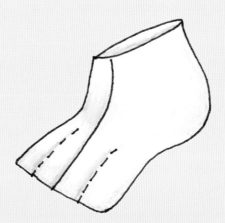

2 Refold the feet with seams together, then pin and stitch the toes closed.

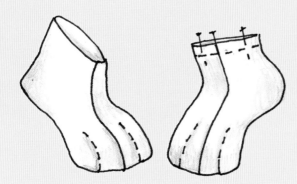

3 Reverse the feet. Topstitch along the markings. Stuff the feet and sew across the top.

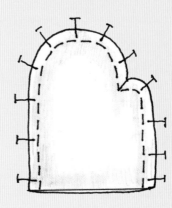

4 Pin and sew the main fabric and the contrast fabric for the hand with right sides together. Repeat for the other hand. Clip the thumb corners.

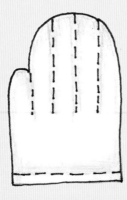

5 Reverse the hands. Topstitch along the markings.

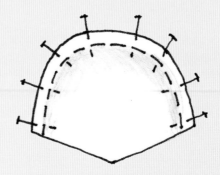

6 Pin and stitch one main fabric ear and one contrast ear with right sides together. Repeat for the other ear. Reverse.

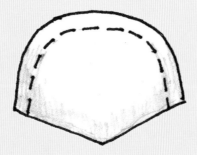

7 Topstitch the ears ¼" (6 mm) from the outside edge. Fold a tuck in each ear and stitch to hold in place.

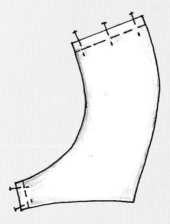

8 Pin and sew the side heads at top and neck with right sides together.

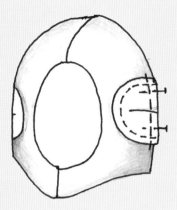

9 Pin and sew the ears to the side heads at markings with right sides together so that contrast fabric side is facing forward.

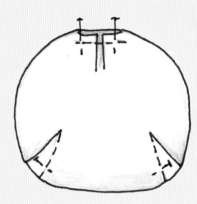

10 Pin and sew the darts of the lower face with right sides together.

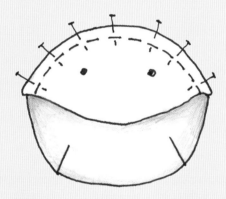

11 Pin and stitch the upper face to the lower face with right sides together. Insert the eyes at the markings, following the package instructions.

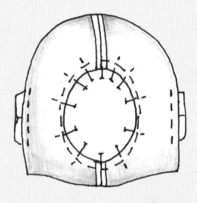

12 Pin and sew the face into the face opening with right sides together.

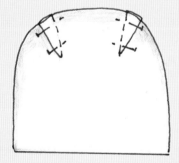

13 Pin and sew the darts in the back head with right sides together.

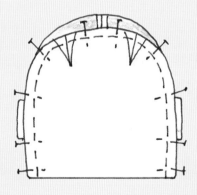

14 Pin and sew the back head to the front with right sides together, catching the ears in the seam. Reverse.

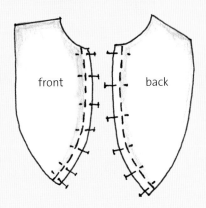

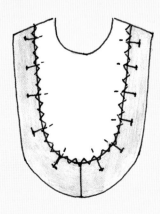

15 Pin and sew the fronts together and the backs together at the centers.

16 Pin the front panel over the center front and zigzag-stitch around the edges. Pin and sew the shoulder seams with right sides together.

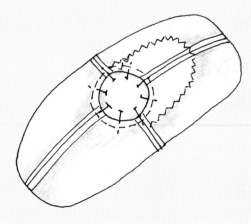

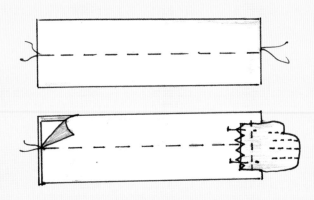

17 Pin and stitch the head to the body opening with right sides together. Make sure the face front aligns with the body front.

18 Machine-baste the center of two arms/legs with wrong sides together, four times. Topstitch the hands and feet to one end of each strip.

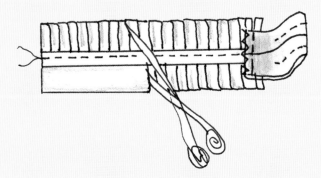

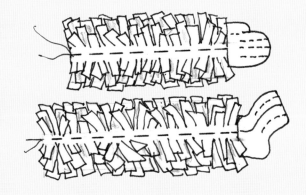

19 Slash from the ends almost up to the stitching every ¼" (6 mm).

20 Pull the basting thread to gather the legs to 8½" (21.5 cm) and the arms to 9" (23 cm).

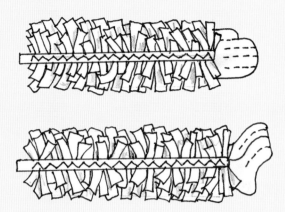

21 Zigzag-stitch the cording over the gathers for the entire length of the arms and legs.

22 Baste the unfinished edge of the arms and legs to the right side of the back body at markings so they extend inward.

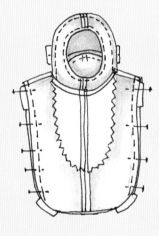

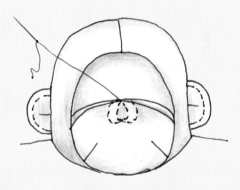

23 Pin the front body over the back body with right sides together and with the arms and legs inside. Pin and stitch the body seam. Leave the lower edge open.

24 Reverse the gorilla. Stuff the head, particularly the face. Fold the nose pleats with wrong sides together and sew along the markings.

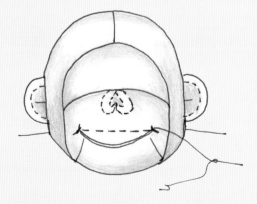

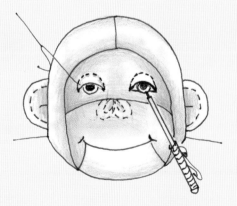

25 Stitch the mouth with embroidery floss, following the pattern markings. Pull the side mouth stitches taut to shape.

26 Hand-sew the eyelids over the eyes. Outline the lower edge of the lids and eyes with permanent marker. Finish stuffing the body. Hand-sew the opening closed.

Simon Snake

Make this snake long or short to fit into the hands of your favorite snake charmer. Fill him with rice so he appears to slither across the playroom floor.

MATERIALS

two pattern pieces

- ⅛ yd. (11.5 cm) fleece in two different colors
- thread
- two ⅛" (3 mm) ball buttons
- 1½" (4 cm) narrow cord
- fiberfill stuffing
- paper
- about 1½ cups (340 g) of rice
- glue
- hand needle

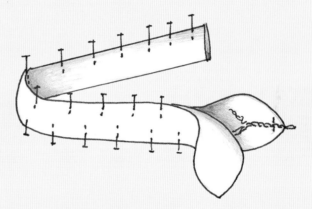

1 Pin narrow cord at the mouth marking so it extends within the body.

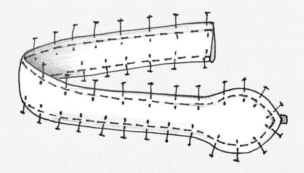

2 Pin and sew the top and bottom body with right sides together, catching the cord in the seam. Leave half of the mouth and tail ends open. Reverse.

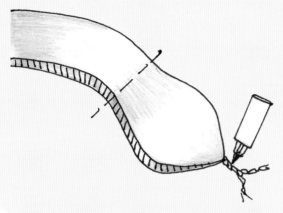

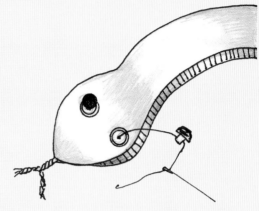

3 Place a dab of glue on the cord ¾" (2 cm) from the face. Let dry and separate the cord ends up to the glued section. Stuff the head with fiberfill and sew closed.

4 Cut two small circles from contrast fleece. Sew a circle and a button eye at one placement mark. Sew through the head to attach the second circle and eye. Secure the thread.

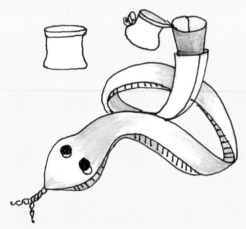

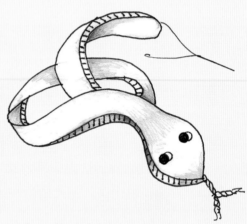

5 Roll the paper to form a funnel and place it in the open end of the snake. Fill the snake three-quarters full.

6 Hand-sew the tail opening closed.

FRENCH KNOT EYES

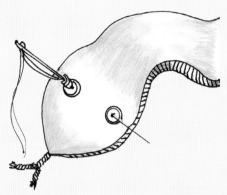

1 Secure the embroidery floss under the eye fleece and bring it to the right side. Wrap the floss around the needle three times and insert the needle in the center of the eye fleece.

2 Pull the needle through the floss, into the snake eye, and out through the other eye. Repeat to make remaining eye. Knot floss under fleece eye.

RATTLE TAIL

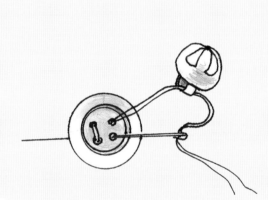

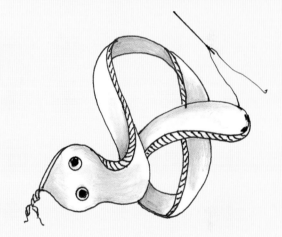

1 Sew a bell onto the flat button.

2 Sew the button and bell to the fleece near the tail end, inside the snake. Sew the snake closed.

Tyrone Tiger

Here's a furry and friendly animal that will pounce right out of the jungle, into a playroom, and straight into your heart!

MATERIALS

six pattern pieces

- ½ yd. (45.5 cm) fleece
- 5" x 4" (12.5 x 10 cm) fleece remnant for ears
- thread
- two ½" (1.5 cm) snap-in eyes
- polyester fiberfill
- pink and black embroidery floss
- powdered blush and brush
- black permanent marker
- hand needle
- long needle

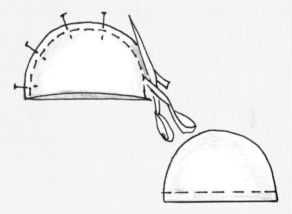

1 Pin and sew the ears with right sides together, leaving the bottom open. Trim and reverse. Stitch across the bottom edge. Clip the seam allowance at the notch.

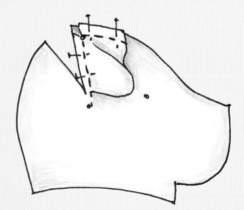

2 Pin the inner ear (contrast fabric) to the right side of the head. Pivot at the notch and continue pinning to the dart opening. Stitch.

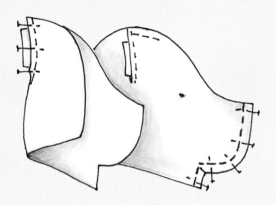

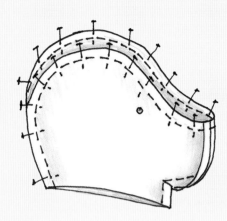

3 Fold and sew the head darts closed with right sides together, catching the ears in the seam. Pin and stitch the chin with right sides together. Clip the curve.

4 Finger-press the chin seam open. Pin and sew the head center to the head sides, with right sides together.

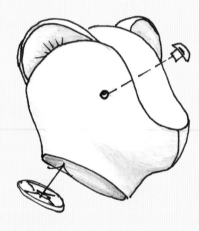

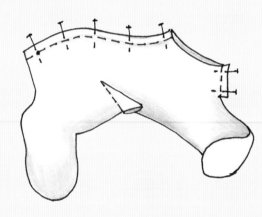

5 Snip a small hole at the eye markings. Turn the head right side out. Push the eyes into the holes and snap the pieces together. Refer to the package instructions.

6 Sew the body darts with right sides together. Pin and sew the top of the body pieces and the small front seam, with right sides together.

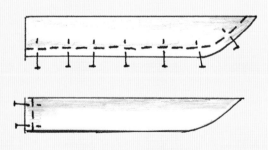

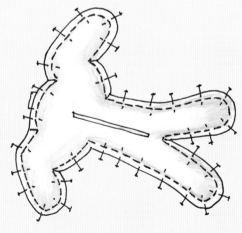

7 Fold the tail in half lengthwise with right sides together. Pin and sew the side and curved edge. Reverse the tail and stitch across the unfinished end.

8 Sew the tail onto the underbody at the marking. Pin and sew the body to the underbody with the tail tucked inside and the right sides together. Stretch the bottom slightly to fit the body. Clip the curves.

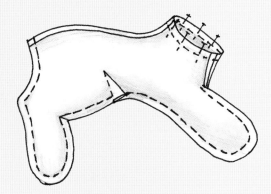

9 Finger-press the back and front seams open. Slip the head into the body with right sides together. Pin and sew the neck seam. Reverse the tiger through the bottom opening.

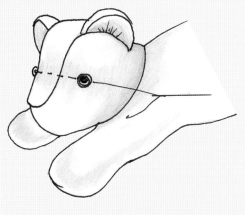

10 Stuff the head firmly. Connect and sink the eyes by taking several stitches through the head with a long needle and double thread. Pull the thread taut.

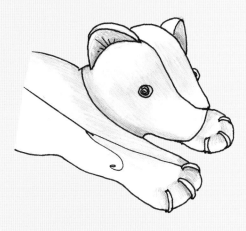

11 Stuff the front paws. Stitch through the front dot marking and around the edge of the paws with two strands of embroidery floss. Repeat two more times.

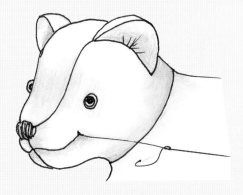

12 Satin-stitch the nose and straight-stitch the mouth with embroidery floss.

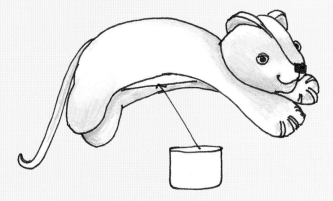

13 Stuff the legs moderately firm. Stuff the body lightly so the tiger is floppy. Hand-sew the opening closed.

14 Dust the inner ears with powdered blush. Outline the eyes with permanent marker.

Harriet Hedgehog

This little hedgehog isn't prickly at all—as a matter of fact, she's as soft and cuddly as can be. Make more in different sizes to start a hedgehog family!

MATERIALS

three pattern pieces

- two ¼ yd. (23 cm) fleece in different colors
- thread
- polyester fiberfill
- two ½" (1.5 cm) flat mother-of-pearl buttons
- two small beads
- embroidery floss
- black permanent marker
- ⅝" (1.5 cm)-wide masking tape
- hand needle

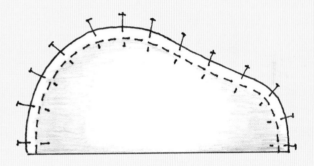

1 Pin and sew the top edge of the bodies with right sides together.

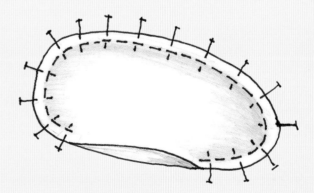

2 Pin and sew the bottom to the body with right sides together, leaving an opening for the stuffing. Reverse.

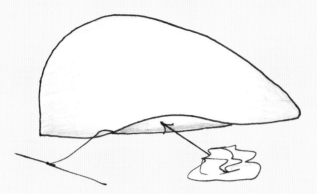

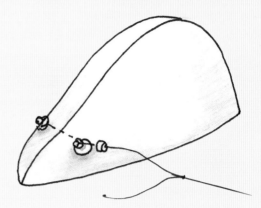

3 Stuff the body firmly and sew the opening closed.

4 Sew one button with a bead over it at the eye-placement marking. Run the thread through the body and attach the other button/bead. Pull taut to sink the eyes slightly.

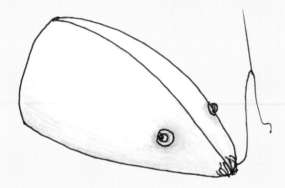

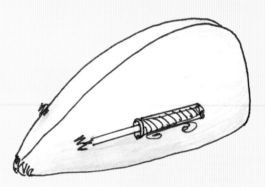

5 Satin-stitch the nose at the markings. Pull the stitches taut to create dimension.

6 To make embroidered eyes (safer for babies), take several satin stitches at the placement marks. Dot the center of the stitches with the marker.

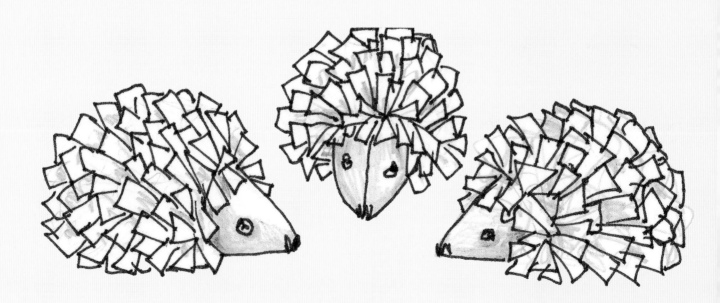

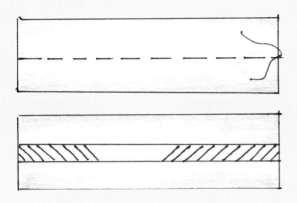

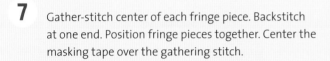

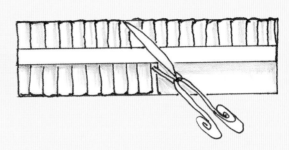

7 Gather-stitch center of each fringe piece. Backstitch at one end. Position fringe pieces together. Center the masking tape over the gathering stitch.

8 Cut strips every ½" (1.5 cm) up to and on each side of the masking tape to create spikes. Remove the tape and separate the strips.

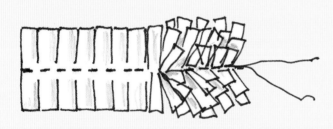

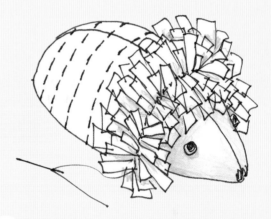

9 Working on each strip separately, pull the gathering stitches from the loose end.

10 Hand-stitch the strips to the body from side to side to completely cover the top. Stitch directly over the gathering stitches.

Peter Panda

Everyone loves a panda, and this stuffed version is no exception. Just look at the sweet eyes and gentle smile. A big hug is all that this little guy needs!

MATERIALS

ten pattern pieces

- two ¼ yd. (23 cm) black and white fleece
- small remnant of white felt
- thread
- polyester fiberfill
- two ¾" (2 cm) flat buttons
- black embroidery floss
- hand needle

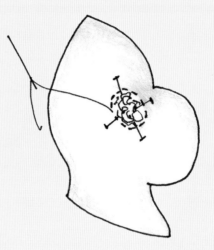

1 Center and hand-sew the wrong side of the eye patches to the right side of the front heads at the marking.

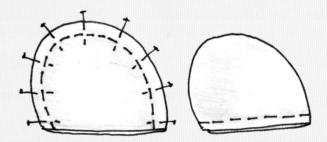

2 With right sides together, pin and sew the ears around the curve. Trim the seam allowance and reverse. Stitch across the bottom.

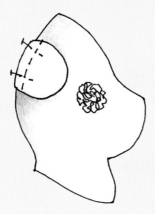

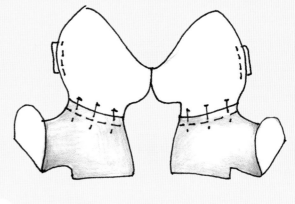

3 Pin and stitch the ears to the front heads between markings.

4 With right sides together, pin and stitch the front heads to the front upper bodies.

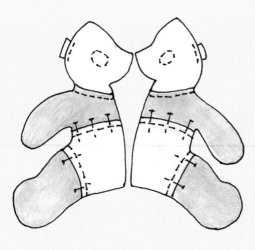

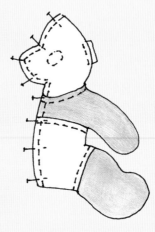

5 Pin and stitch the front lower bodies to the front legs, then pin and stitch the front upper bodies to the front lower bodies to create right and left front sides.

6 With right sides together, pin and stitch the center front seam from top to bottom.

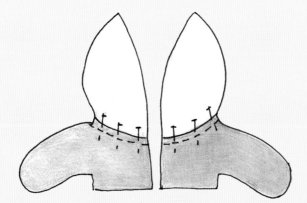

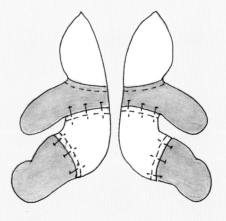

7 With right sides together, pin and stitch the back heads to the back upper bodies.

8 Pin and stitch the back lower bodies to the back legs. Pin and stitch the back upper bodies to the back lower bodies to create right and left back sides.

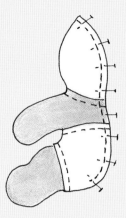 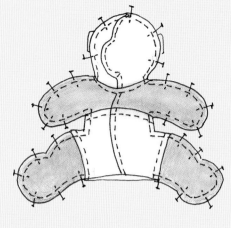

9 With right sides together, pin and stitch the center back seam from top to bottom.

10 With right sides together, pin and sew the panda front to the panda back. Leave the bottom open for stuffing. Clip and reverse.

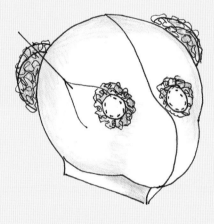 

11 Stuff the head firmly. Sew the white eye circles onto the eye patches.

12 Sew the button onto the eye circles. Pull the thread through the head to sink the eyes slightly.

 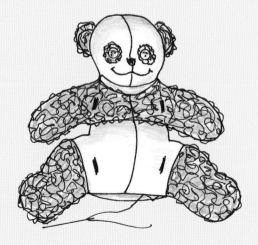

13 Satin-stitch the nose with floss. Straight-stitch the mouth, following the markings, and pull thread through head to shape. Take short straight stitches under the chin for shape, and pull taut.

14 Stuff the body lightly with arms and legs three-quarters full. Sew opening closed. Take short straight stitches at the arm and leg markings to create joints.

Water Animals

Everyone loves the charming animals that frolic in the sea.

Maybe it's because we secretly wish we could swim right alongside them. Well, perhaps we can't join them underwater, but there's no reason they can't join us here on land. It's easy to create a sea habitat right in your own home by making two or three—or maybe all five!—of these surprisingly simple-to-sew fleece creatures.

Welcome a waddling penguin from the South Pole and a polar bear cub from the North Pole—and an octopus, walrus, and turtle from the watery regions in between. Each of these animals has an extra-special charming detail. The octopus wears a wonderful green hat (although the walrus could wear it, too). The jaunty turtle sports a small ruffle and flowers, and the walrus couldn't be cuter with his droopy yarn whiskers and satiny, faux-ivory tusks!

Pablo Polar Bear

Just look at the twinkle in the faceted button eyes of this spunky polar bear!
He looks full of sweet mischief and very cuddly and warm—no matter
how cold it is outside.

MATERIALS

six pattern pieces

- ¼ yd. (23 cm) fleece
- thread
- polyester fiberfill
- embroidery floss
- two ball buttons
- hand needle
- black permanent marker

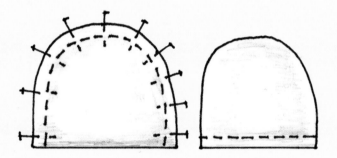

1 Pin and sew the ears and tail with right sides together. Reverse and sew across the lower edge.

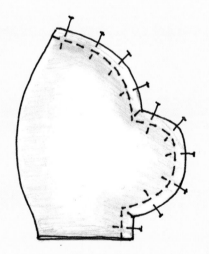

2 Pin and sew the face with right sides together. Clip the corner at the chin.

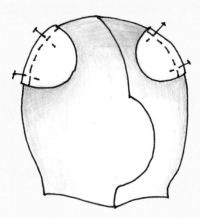

3 Pin and sew the ears onto the face at the markings.

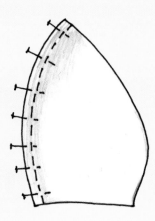

4 Pin and sew the center back head with right sides together.

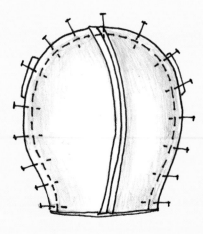

5 Pin and sew the face to the back head with right sides together. Reverse.

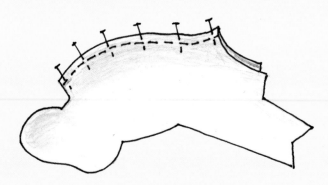

6 Pin and sew the upper body center back seam with right sides together.

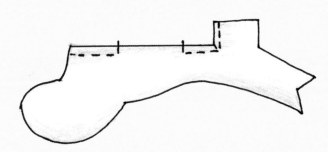

7 Pin and sew the underbody seam between the markings with right sides together. Leave center unstitched.

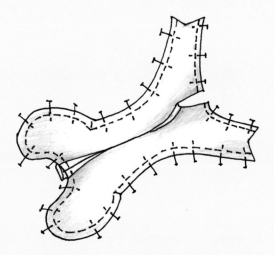

8 Place the tail at the marking facing inward. Pin and sew the upper body to the underbody with right sides together. Leave the front edge of the front paws unstitched.

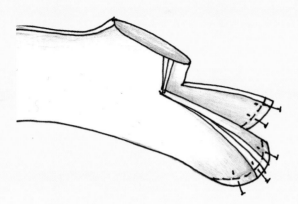

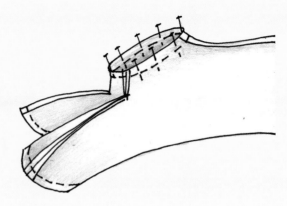

9 Fold the front paws so the seams are together. Pin and sew.

10 With right sides together, insert the head into the neck opening. Pin and sew. Reverse the polar bear. Stuff the head and front paws firmly.

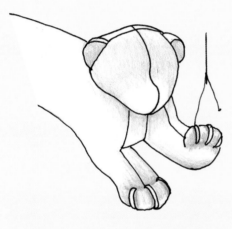

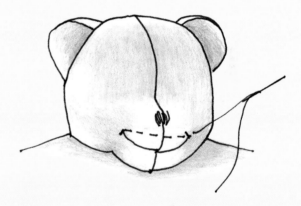

11 Take three straight stitches over the edge of the front paws with embroidery floss. Pull taut, but not tight, to create shape.

12 Satin-stitch the nose and straight-stitch the mouth at the markings. Pull the stitches taut to shape.

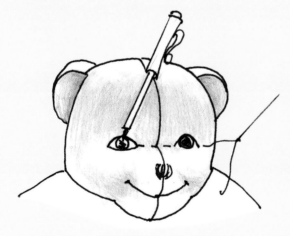

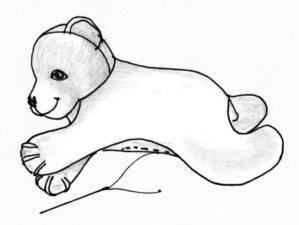

13 Sew the buttons at the eye markings, pulling stitches through the head to sink the eyes. Darken and outline the eyes with permanent marker.

14 Stuff the remainder of the polar bear and hand-stitch the opening closed.

Olivia Octopus

One of the extra-special things about this cheery two-tone octopus is that she has lots of long buttoned arms for squeezing and hugging—eight in all!

MATERIALS

five pattern pieces

- ⁵⁄₈ yd. (57 cm) fleece
- ¼ yd. (23 cm) contrast fleece
- thread (white, fleece-colored, and button-colored)
- polyester fiberfill
- two 1" (2.5 cm)-diameter flat buttons
- fifty-six ¾" (2 cm)-diameter flat buttons or white fabric paint
- hand needle
- black permanent marker

For hat materials and instructions, see page 108.

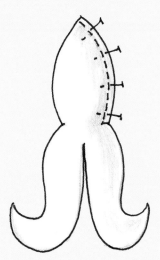

1 With right sides together, pin and sew the head section of two body pieces.

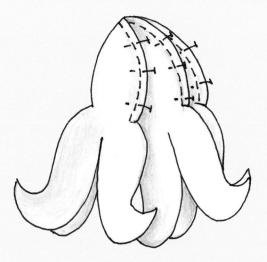

2 Pin and sew the remaining body pieces with right sides together as in step 1 to form the closed octopus top.

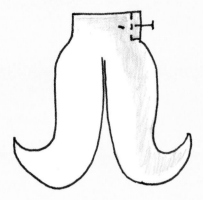

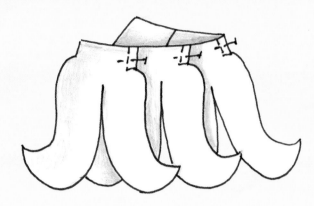

3 With right sides together, pin and sew the body section (between markings) of two leg facing pieces.

4 Pin and sew the remaining leg facing pieces with right sides together as in step 3 to form the closed octopus bottom.

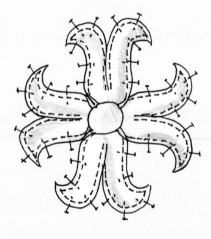

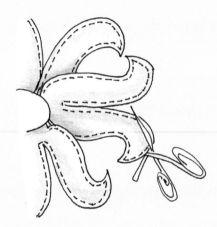

5 With right sides together and seams aligned, pin and sew the octopus body to the facing around the perimeter of the tentacles.

6 Trim the seams and clip the curves.

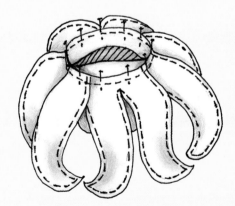

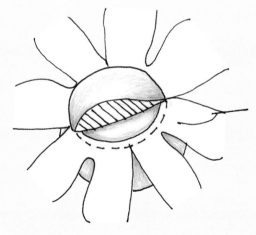

7 With right sides together, pin and stitch the bottom to the opening, leaving about one-third unstitched. Reverse the octopus.

8 Stuff the head firmly. Stuff the tentacles softly, pushing the stuffing all the way to the tips of the tentacles.

9 Hand-sew the opening closed.

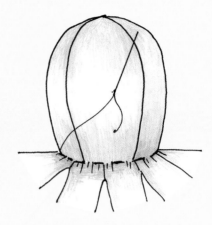

10 With a double strand of thread, straight-stitch around the head at the beginning of the tentacles to create shape. Make small, even stitches. Pull the stitches taut.

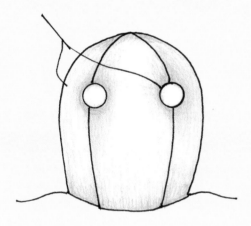

11 Hand-sew eye circles at the markings.

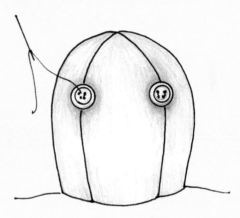

12 Sew larger buttons over the circles. Stitch one button hole with white thread and the others with button-colored thread.

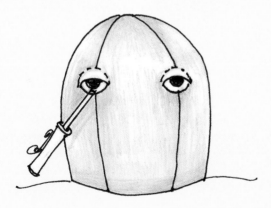

13 Hand-sew eyelids over the eyes. Outline the lower edge of the eyelids with permanent marker.

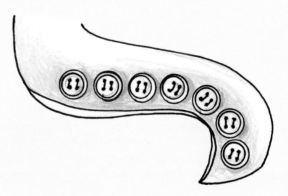

14 Sew seven buttons to the bottom side of each tentacle. As a shortcut, you can paint circles with white fabric paint instead of using buttons.

Polly Penguin

How can you resist this adorable penguin—with her quirky shape, silly waddle, and black-and-white birthday suit? She's sure to quickly become a take-everywhere friend!

MATERIALS

nine pattern pieces

- ¼ yd. (23 cm) black fleece
- ¼ yd. (23 cm) white fleece
- thread
- polyester fiberfill
- two black ball buttons (or beads)
- hand needle
- fleece remnant for tongue

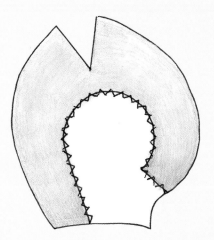

1 Zigzag-topstitch the wrong side of the faces onto the right side of the heads.

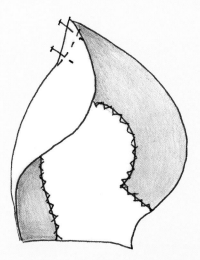

2 Pin and stitch the head darts with right sides together.

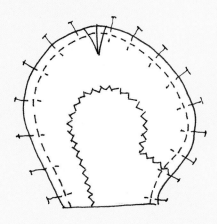

3 Pin and stitch the heads with right sides together.

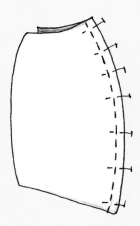

4 Pin and stitch the center back seam with right sides together.

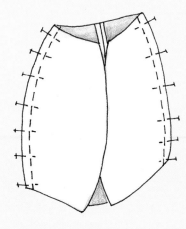

5 Pin and sew the fronts to the back at the side seams with right sides together.

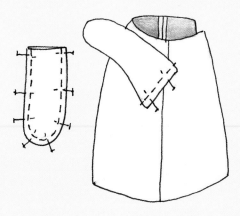

6 Pin and sew one white and one black wing with right sides together. Repeat with the remaining wings. Reverse. Pin the wings to the body at the marked locations.

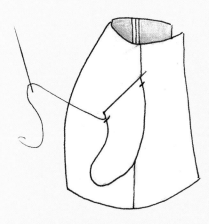

7 Sew the wings to the body and fold them over the stitching. Tack the wings down on the sides near the folds.

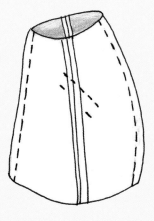

8 Sew the center front seam with right sides together.

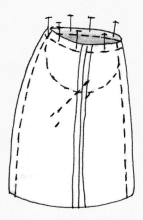

9 Insert the head into the body with right sides together. Pin and sew.

10 Reverse the penguin.

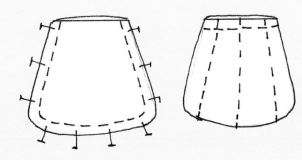

11 Pin and sew each foot with right sides together. Reverse. Topstitch along the markings.

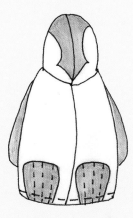

12 Pin the top of the feet to the bottom edge of the body front and stitch.

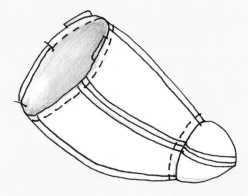

13 Pin and stitch the body to the bottom with right sides together and feet tucked inside, leaving an opening. Reverse. Stuff the body and head. Hand-stitch the opening closed.

14 Attach the eyes, pulling the thread inside the head to sink them slightly. Center tongue inside the beak. Stitch across center of both layers onto face at marking and fold down the beak.

Tilly Turtle

Here's a soft-shelled turtle that doesn't need any camouflage! Go ahead and choose fleece in bright, bold colors that will cheer up the room she calls home.

MATERIALS

seven pattern pieces

- ⅓ yd. (30.5 cm) fleece for turtle shell
- ¼ yd. (23 cm) fleece for turtle bottom
- fleece remnants for ruffle and eyes
- thread
- polyester fiberfill
- embroidery floss
- hand needle

For flower materials and instructions, see page 109.

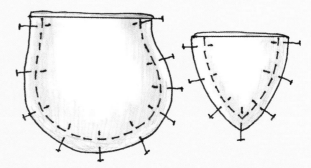

1 Pin and sew two feet and a tail with right sides together, leaving the top edge open. Reverse all pieces.

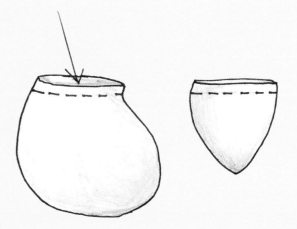

2 Stuff the feet and tail lightly and baste across the top edges.

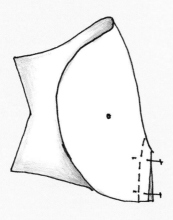

3 With right sides together, pin and sew the mouth darts.

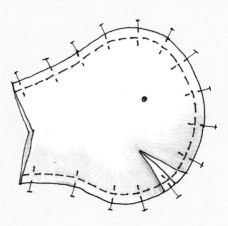

4 With right sides together, pin and sew the head, leaving the neck edge open.

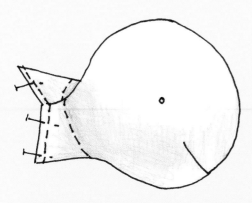

5 Stuff the head firmly. Sew the bottom edge closed along the pattern marking.

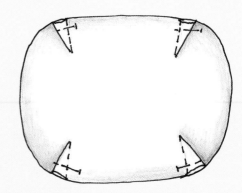

6 With right sides together, pin and sew the four shell darts.

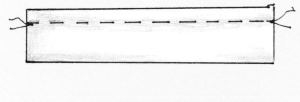

7 Baste along one long edge of the ruffle. Pull the thread to gather the ruffle so it's equal in length to the shell perimeter.

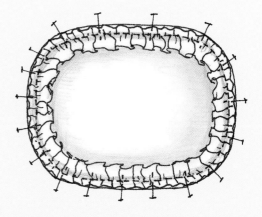

8 With right sides together, pin and sew the ruffle to the shell, adjust gathers to fit, and overlap ends near turtle back.

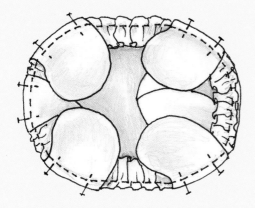

9 Pin and sew the feet, head, and tail to the shell over the ruffle at markings so they extend inward.

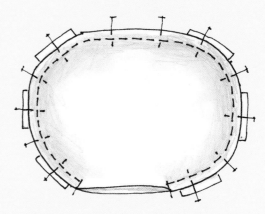

10 With right sides together, pin and sew the bottom to the shell, catching the feet, tail, head, and ruffle in the seam. Leave one side between the feet open.

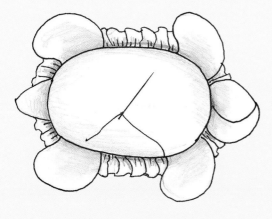

11 Stuff the turtle body and hand-sew the opening closed.

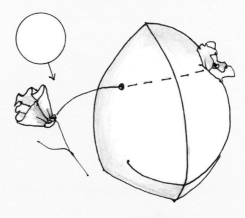

12 Pinch the center of the eyes and stitch to the head at markings with several stitches and black floss.

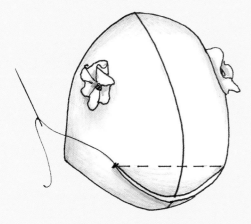

13 Sew one long straight stitch along the darts to make the mouth. Pull the thread through the inside of the head to shape the mouth. Knot the thread at each side.

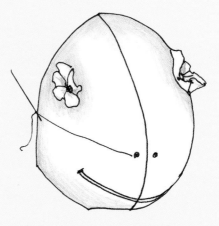

14 Sew two or three small straight stitches at each nose marking.

Wally Walrus

Here's a fleece fellow that's very easy to fall in love with. Just wrap your arms around him. He's big and strong and ready to play!

MATERIALS

eight pattern pieces

- ½ yd. (45.5 cm) fleece
- remnant of white satin for tusks
- remnant of white fleece for eyes
- thread
- embroidery floss
- polyester fiberfill
- ⁵/₈" (1.5 cm)-diameter ball buttons
- hand needle
- fabric glue

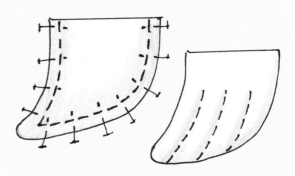

1 Pin and stitch the flippers with right sides together. Reverse and topstitch along the markings.

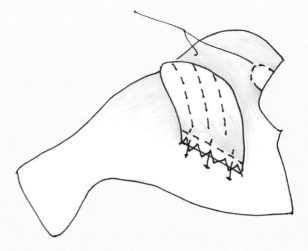

2 Pin the flippers on the right side of the bodies along the placement markings and zigzag-stitch over the raw edges. Hand-stitch the eyes on the right side of the head at the placement markings.

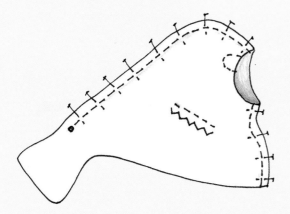

3 Pin and stitch the bodies with right sides together at the front and top.

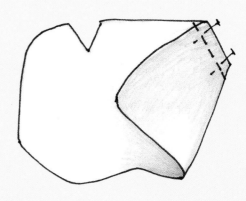

4 Pin and stitch the upper muzzle darts with right sides together.

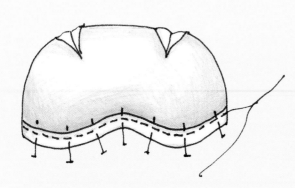

5 Fold the lower edge of the upper muzzle top to the wrong side and hand-stitch it to upper hem.

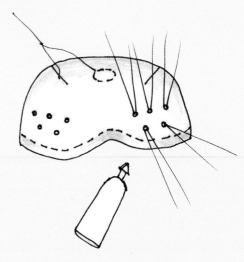

6 Hand-stitch the nose in place. Cut the floss into 4" (10 cm) lengths. Thread floss through the muzzle at each marking and double knot to secure. Dab glue on the wrong side of the whisker dots.

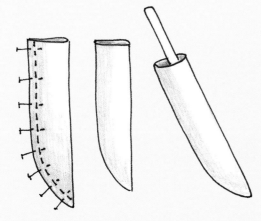

7 Pin and sew the tusks with wrong sides together. Reverse and stuff firmly.

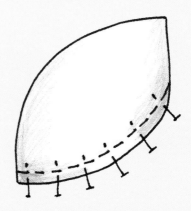

8 Pin and sew the under muzzle with right sides together.

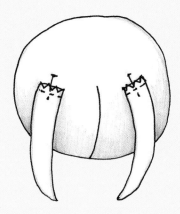

9   Hand-stitch the tusks onto the right side of the under muzzle at the markings.

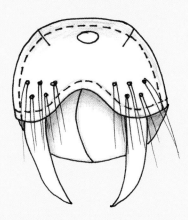

10   Pin and stitch the wrong side of the upper muzzle over the right side of the under muzzle.

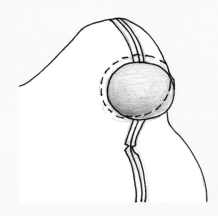

11   Insert the muzzle into the head opening so right sides are together. Pin and stitch.

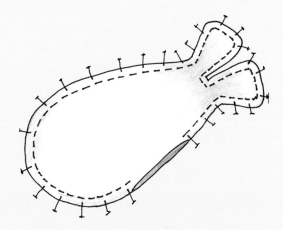

12   Pin and sew the underbody to the body with right sides together. Leave an opening along one side. Clip the corners. Reverse.

13   Stuff the body and hand-sew the opening closed.

14   Sew the button eyes in place. Add fiberfill under each side of the muzzle to make cheeks. Straight-stitch from the nose to the bottom of the upper muzzle and secure the upper muzzle to the under muzzle.

Extra-Special Touches

Here are a few fun and easy accessories that you can make!

Choose whichever one—or two or three!—you'd like. Don't be afraid to experiment by adding your own creative touches. These finishing touches are a perfect way to use any leftover fleece scraps. You can make matching or contrasting pillows and blankets for the animals from scraps, too—a great project for a child who wants to help! Personalize your extras with a little decorative embroidery.

Here are three simple accessories designed with Hanna Horse, Olivia Octopus, and Tilly Turtle in mind—but you can mix and match the accessories and animals however you'd like. You'll find the patterns for these accessories in the front of the book. They're all easy to sew and will add an extra-special finishing touch to your fabulous fleece creature! So, get creative—and have fun!

RIDING SADDLE AND BLANKET

Place this comfy saddle on the back of your Hanna Horse (page 44),
and she'll look like she just came out of the stable, ready for a ride.

MATERIALS

two pattern pieces

- three contrast pieces of fleece 4" x 7" (10 x 18 cm) for blanket (1) and saddle (2)
- 9" (23 cm)-long piece of ½" (1.3 cm)-wide bias tape
- two 1" (2.5 cm) D-rings
- two ¼" (6 mm) gold beads
- 10" (25.5 cm)-long ¾" (2 cm)-wide hook-and-loop tape
- sewing thread
- hand needle

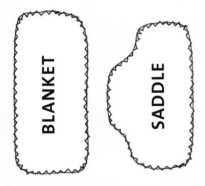

1   Pin the two saddle pieces with the wrong sides together. Zigzag-stitch around the outside of the blanket and saddle.

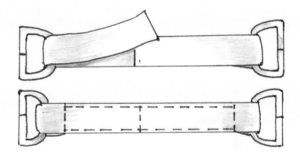

2   Slip D-rings on both ends of the bias tape. Fold over the ends to secure the D-rings and stitch. Machine-stitch above the D-rings and along the outside edges.

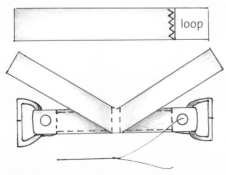

3   Cut a 9" (23 cm) hook side and a 2" (5 cm) loop (soft) side of tape. Zigzag them together. Center and stitch the hook-and-loop strip onto the stirrups. Sew gold beads on stirrups.

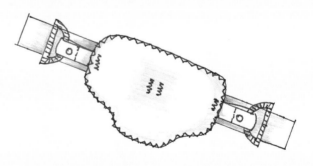

4   Center the saddle over the stirrups. Machine-stitch through all the layers in the center of the saddle and at the lower edges.

OUTRAGEOUS HAT

Only an extra-special critter, like Olivia Octopus (page 90), would wear such an outrageous cap!
Make this in matching or contrasting colors—and tip it just a bit for a jaunty look.

MATERIALS

six pattern pieces

- 12" (30.5 cm) fleece remnant
- two remnants for flower
- 3" x ¼" (7.5 cm x 6 mm) fleece remnant for flower center
- sewing thread
- hand needle

1 Stitch the hat brim to the hat top with right sides together.

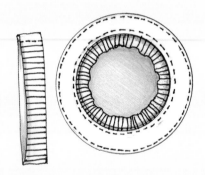

2 Stitch the narrow ends of the band with right sides together. Pin and stitch the band to the brim with right sides together.

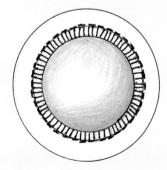

3 Fold the band over the seam to cover it. Stitch-in-the-ditch (directly over the previous stitching) to secure the band to the brim. Trim seam allowance close to stitching. Reverse.

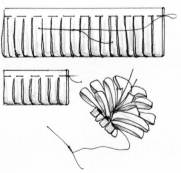

4 Fold flower pieces in half and baste top edge. Cut from fold to stitching every ¼" (6 mm). Pull thread to make a circle, and knot. Stitch layers together, including flower center. Attach flower and leaves to hat.

FUN FLOWER

Tilly Turtle (page 98) has the perfect topper—a bright and sunny flower with
a fluffy center. It's just the right kind of frilly extra for her ruffled shell.

MATERIALS

one pattern piece

- fleece remnant
- pom-pom
- sewing thread
- hand needle

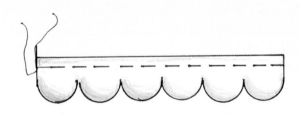

1   Baste the top edge of the flower.

2   Pull and knot the thread to shape the flower. Secure with a few hand stitches.

3   Sew the pom-pom in the center of the flower.

4   Sew the flower onto the turtle shell.

Glossary

BASTE: to temporarily hold fabric layers together by sewing with long stitches. Basting stitches are sewn on a single layer of fabric in preparation for gathering the fabric.

CLIP: to cut slits into the seam allowance almost to the line of stitching, working with only the tips of the scissors. Clipping eases a curved seam and helps a corner to lie smooth.

DART: a stitched fold that tapers from the fabric edge to a point inside the piece to create shape

EASE: to smooth fabric within the stitching

EMBROIDERY: decorative stitches worked by hand or machine

FINGER-PRESS: to fold a seam open with your fingers

GATHERING: the process of pulling up basting stitches to make a section of fabric shorter, forming small, soft folds

MARK: to transfer important construction symbols from the pattern onto the fabric

SEAM ALLOWANCE: the amount of fabric between the cut edge and the stitched seam

SELVAGE: the narrow, finished edge of the fabric

SLIP STITCH: an almost invisible hand stitch used to sew together two folded edges together or one folded edge onto a flat fabric surface

STITCH-IN-THE-DITCH: to machine-stitch directly over an already-stitched seam to hold fabric in place without allowing the stitching to show

TACK: to make small hand stitches in one area to secure, reinforce, or strengthen seams or embroidery

TOPSTITCH: to machine-stitch on the right side of the project parallel to a seam or folded edge

ZIGZAG STITCH: a back-and-forth machine stitch that forms a strong seam or decorative finish

Sources of Supply

Here are some of the sources of materials for the projects in this book. There are many others to choose from—both retail and online—for fleece, thread, yarn, animal eyes, beads, notions, and supplies.

RETAIL SOURCES

For fabric, thread, yarn, and notions

Banksville Designer Fabrics
115 New Canaan Avenue
Norwalk, CT 06850
1-203-845-7966
www.banksvilledesignerfabrics.com

Jo-Ann Fabric and Craft Stores
1-888-739-4120
www.joann.com

For yarn, animal eyes, beads, and craft supplies

A. C. Moore
1-866-342-8802
www.acmoore.com

Michaels Stores Inc.
1-800-642-4235
www.michaels.com

ONLINE SOURCES

For fleece fabric

Denver Fabrics
1-800-468-0602
www.denverfabrics.com

Fabricland
1-908-755-4700
www.fabricland.com

The Fleece Lady
1-909-223-3533
www.fleecelady.com

J & O Fabric Center
1-856-663-2121
www.jandofabrics.com

For animal eyes and notions

BJ's Craft Supplies
361-286-3366
www.bjcraftsupplies.com

Craft Bits
44 (0) 173-356-6617
www.craftbits.co.uk

Sunshine Discount Crafts
1-800-729-2878
www.sunshinecrafts.com

CATALOG AND ONLINE SOURCES

For thread, yarn, animal eyes, and notions

Atlanta Thread & Supply Company
1-800-847-1001
www.atlantathread.com

Home-Sew Inc.
1-800-344-4739
www.homesew.com

Newark Dressmaker Supply
1-800-736-6783
www.newarkdress.com

About the Author

When Linda Carr couldn't find a quality doll for her young daughter, she began designing her own soft-body dolls.

As she developed her home-based doll and toy design business, she caught the attention of the merchandisers at *Vogue Patterns* and began a successful relationship. For more than twenty-five years, Linda has designed some of the best-selling Vogue Craft patterns.

Today, she continues to design and produce commercial patterns for *Vogue*, including keepsake-quality dolls, doll accessories, stuffed animals (including the Vogue Bear Collection), home décor, and fashion accessories. She has collaborated to create several licensed patterns, including many for Jim Henson's Muppets, Cabbage Patch Kids, and the World Wildlife Federation.

A former art teacher, Linda created all the drawings and patterns for this book. She lives with her husband in Guilford, Connecticut.